A Christian Woman book
Alone with God

Jean Holl became a Christian early in life and grew up in a Baptist church in Bromley. She and her husband Peter moved to the Medway Towns in 1968, and are involved in leadership and teaching in their parish church. They have four children. This book developed from a series of talks given by the author on the quiet time. She is also contributor to an earlier Christian Woman book, *Creativity*.

GW00729902

Christian Woman Books

Series Editor: Gail Lawther

Other titles in preparation

Alone with God

Making the most of your quiet time

JEAN HOLL

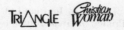

First published 1986
Triangle
SPCK
Holy Trinity Church
Marylebone Road
London NW1 4DU

ACKNOWLEDGEMENTS

Unless otherwise stated, Bible quotations are from
the Revised Standard Version of the Bible, copyrighted
1946, 1952 © 1971, 1973 by the Division of Christian Education
of the National Council of the Churches of Christ in the USA,
and used by permission.

British Library Cataloguing in Publication Data

Holl, Jean
    Alone with God : making the most of your quiet time.
    — (Christian woman books)
    1. Prayer
    I. Title   II. Series
    248.3'2   BV210.2

    ISBN 0-281-04228-4

Typeset by Inforum Ltd
Printed in Great Britain by
Hazell, Watson & Viney Limited
Member of the BPCC Group
Aylesbury, Bucks

CONTENTS

CONTENTS

Series Editor's Foreword

Christian women are developing a new awareness of the way our faith touches every part of our lives. Women who have always lived in a Christian environment are facing up to the important issues in the world around them. Women who have found in Christ a new direction for living are seeking to sort out the problems that are hampering their spiritual growth. And many women are rediscovering the joy in using their God-given talents, in their relationships with God and with other people, and in their spiritual lives and worship. *Christian Woman* magazine has been privileged to be part of this learning process.

As a result of this deepening awareness and commitment to Christianity, many books have been published which help women to sort out what God can do for them as women, as wives, as career people, as mothers, as single women. Most of these books however have been rooted in the American culture; this *Christian Woman* series has come into being because we believe it is important that we have books that talk our own language, and are relevant to everyday life in our own culture.

Each book in this series will deal with some aspect of living as a Christian woman in today's world. I am delighted that we have been able to be part of the blossoming of God's church in this way. We hope that the books will help you as a Christian woman to overcome problems, enrich your life and your relationships, learn more of God, think through important issues, enjoy your femininity, make wise choices, and deepen your commitment to Jesus Christ.

In these books we have invited people to share what they have learned about living as Christians. Not everyone will agree with all the ideas expressed in each book, but I know that you will find every book in the series interesting and thought-provoking.

Books change people lives – perhaps these books will change your life.

GAIL LAWTHER

1

God's Invitation

My husband Peter and I were enjoying a meal of spaghetti bolognese with a young couple from our church. After we had washed up and were sitting down with our coffee and chatting generally, the subject of quiet times came up, and the husband leaned forward and asked us 'What exactly do you two do in your quiet times?' A bit taken aback at such a forthright question, we briefly shared our experiences, and the rest of the evening was spent talking about our individual relationships with God.

Later that week another young wife called in for a cup of coffee. She had just left work to have her first baby, and again, the subject of quiet times arose. I remember encouraging her to spend as much time with the Lord as she could before the baby came, and told her some of the things I found helpful in my own quiet times.

Those two conversations set me thinking about this important subject, and I began searching the Bible to see what God had to say. I shared my initial findings with our house group, then later Peter and I jointly gave talks to a group in church, which eventually led to this book. It is partly aimed at those who have recently become Christians, and is also relevant to people who have been Christians for a while, maybe even a long time, yet find their quiet times boring and lacking a vital sense of the Lord's presence.

At this point you may be asking yourself, 'What is a quiet time?', and wondering how a whole book can be devoted to such a subject! Basically, what I mean by our quiet time is the time we spend alone with God each day, getting to know him, giving him our worship, reading and studying the Scriptures, and praying. Sadly, many who have been Christians for a long time are still muddling through a quick five or ten minutes of prayer and Bible reading, simply because no one has taken the trouble to sit down with them and show them what else to do. Without such guidance, new Christians may enthusiastically start reading the Bible at Genesis and then wonder why they get bogged down a few chapters later. They try praying, but because no one has really shown them how to pray, that too peters out, and they are left with a guilty feeling that they are not doing what every other Christian in their church is faithfully doing each day – or so they think! The truth is that many Christians get so little out of their quiet times, or don't even have one at all, that they are ashamed to admit it.

On the whole there is very little teaching on how to spend time with the Lord, and on what we can actually do during this important daily meeting. The purpose of this book is to provide just that – to give you as a seeking Christian a variety of suggestions on what you can do; but more importantly, to show you how joyful and fulfilling quiet times can be, and how they are the way in which we enter the very presence of God himself.

When I began seriously thinking about this subject I discovered, to my surprise, that quiet times are not just a matter of reading the Bible and praying. In fact I have found between thirty and forty suggestions, or elements, that can be included in this time alone with the Lord. As I began to experiment and try many of these new elements for myself, my devotions quickly became far more meaningful, and almost for the first time I found I was able to break through barriers and begin to sense the presence of God, especially as I learned the importance and value of praise and worship.

This book, therefore, is not just for you to read, but to experiment with, and to put into practice some of the suggestions that may be new to you. There will also be practical ideas to help you develop some of the things that may already form part of your devotional time. If you are a new Christian, some of the terminology may be hard to understand, so I have included an explanation at the end of the chapters where necessary.

One of the first things to bear in mind is that each one of us has received a personal invitation from the King of kings and Lord of lords – and by personal I mean that he actually calls *you* by name. God did this to a very young lad, back in Old Testament times (1 Samuel 3.6-9). Samuel had never before heard the Lord call him, and thought it was old Eli the priest. Three times the Lord called Samuel by name and each time the boy ran to Eli. Then the old priest realised that it was the Lord calling Samuel, and he showed him how to answer the fourth call when it came. In the New Testament we have Jesus describing himself as the good shepherd, and how the sheep hear his voice as he calls them by name (John 10.3). Part of your conversion experience may have involved being taught that your name is now written in the Lamb's Book of Life (Luke 10.20 and Philippians 4.3). So of course the Lord already knows you and your name personally, and he is able to invite you individually to come and meet with him.

How do you feel when you receive an invitation to a friend's party? You are pleased that they've bothered to write; you're flattered to be invited to celebrate with them, and you begin immediately to look forward to the pleasant company, the good food, the enjoyable conversation. You book the date on your calendar to make sure you keep that evening free.

Our Lord longs for us to have this same sense of excitement and anticipation as he invites us into his presence through the means of our quiet times.

God calls us to him whatever our circumstances, and however we are feeling at the time. We may be feeling very low and rather dry spiritually. God's response is already

3

there to meet our need – 'Ho, every one who thirsts, come to the waters', he says through the prophet Isaiah (55.1). The prophet goes on to tell of the wonderful things God plans to do through those who accept his invitation . . . 'a witness to the peoples . . . a commander for the peoples . . . you shall call nations that you know not . . .'

Like guests looking forward to the good food at a party, we may long to be fed spiritually with the deep things of God. There is a beautiful verse in Revelation chapter 3 which tells us that Jesus is knocking on the door of our hearts, wanting to come in and eat with us, to share a meal together. The appeal is made to the individual – 'If anyone . . . opens the door, I will come in to him.' But notice that it is given in the context of a letter written to a church – to Christians, and not to unbelievers. Unfortunately, Jesus describes the church concerned as 'wretched, pitiable, poor, blind and naked'. Is he hinting here that an entire church can be revitalised when its individual members have learned to spend time alone in fellowship with him? As you read and study this book, I hope that you will discover that what starts out as something personal, for your own individual benefit and blessing, eventually ends up by deepening the life of the whole church.

Knowing that the Lord wants to quench our thirst and feed us with good things makes us realise that he actually wants us to find satisfaction in coming into his presence. And that is what quiet times are – accepting the invitation of God and setting time aside in our busy lives to be alone with the one who satisfies: 'My people will be satisfied with my goodness, says the Lord' (Jeremiah 31.14). And who knows what results may follow?

Now you can see that you and I have a personal invitation that needs a response, and on the surface such a request leads us to suppose that our quiet times are for our benefit. It was therefore quite a surprise to me when I discovered for the first time that they are equally important to God. As I studied the Scriptures, this fact became increasingly clear.

4

I first realised this several years ago when my family and I were on holiday on the Isle of Wight. I had experienced a year of depression following the birth of our son and the death of my father within six weeks of each other, and I was just beginning to feel well again. One morning, while Peter took the children for a walk, I picked up my Bible. It was the first time I had done so for many weeks, and I started to read Paul's letter to the Romans. I arrived at verse 11 and found myself reading and re-reading the words: 'For I long to see you, that I may impart some spiritual gift to strengthen you, that is, that we may be mutually encouraged . . .' To begin with it warmed my heart when I realised that God was saying to me 'I long to see you', and that he had spiritual gifts to strengthen me; but then the words 'mutually encouraged' kept going round and round in my head, and although of course Paul was writing here about himself to the Christians in Rome, God used those words that morning to show me something I needed to know. This was the simple but profound fact that quiet times were for his benefit as well as mine. They were as important to God as they were to me, for by my coming into his presence we would mutually encourage and bless each other. It would be a two-way affair. Not only that, I was actually denying the Lord many things by not coming into his presence. Psalm 147 says that 'The Lord takes *pleasure* in those who fear him.' So by absenting myself from his company, I was not only denying myself the pleasure of being with the Lord, but more seriously, denying God the pleasure of being with me.

This may be hard to believe if you are the sort of person who finds it hard to love and accept yourself, or if you feel you are of little value; but the plain truth is that if God went to the trouble and heartache of first creating us and then sending his Son to die for us, then it is only natural that he should want to spend as much time as possible in our company.

Once I realised how important it was to respond to God's

5

personal invitation and make room for him in my busy day, I found Scripture ready to show me why. I found two reasons, in Isaiah and Revelation: 'Worthy art thou, O Lord, our God, to receive glory and honour and power, for thou didst create all things and *for thy pleasure they were created*' (Revelation 4.11, AV). 'Bring my sons and daughters from afar, every one who is called by my name, *whom I created for my glory*, whom I formed and made' (Isaiah 43.7).

I discovered, then, that we were created for his glory and pleasure, and actually made to have fellowship with him. I found this same theme, and also that of our personal invitation, right at the beginning of the Bible, in Genesis 3.9. God was walking in the garden in the cool of the evening with the intention of speaking with Adam and Eve. But they were not at their usual meeting place, and God, naturally, missed their company. So he started looking for them, and calling out, 'Where are you?' He wanted to have a heart-to-heart chat with them, to share himself with them; but they were missing, hiding in the bushes because, having sinned, they now realised they were naked, and they were ashamed to face God.

God wants to say many things to you and me, and to do many things in our lives, but he cannot if we do not give him our time, presence and attention. I imagined the Lord calling to me: 'Where are you, Jean? I want to talk with you, to share my thoughts with you, to bless you, heal you, make you mature.' But where was I? I was busy doing other things, or too tired, and not even thinking about the Lord. I couldn't be bothered to spend time with the King of kings.

Once I saw that my quiet times were for our mutual encouragement and blessing, I began to see too that here was an opportunity for me to *give* to God, instead of always being on the receiving end. This was God's chance to *receive* from me; and as I thought, studied and prayed, I realised that there were many things I could give to God, such as my love, my time, my attention, my presence, my

6

praise and worship – in fact my very self.

God, as our creator, has certain rights, and we deny these to him if we don't set time aside each day to spend with him. Conversely, God is thrilled when we do put him first and plan our day in such a way that we have an opportunity to praise and worship him and be available to hear what he has to say. He loves it! We actually satisfy the deep desires of his heart when we put him first, and in turn we find that mutual giving and receiving results in mutual satisfaction.

This two-way relationship is implied in 2 Chronicles chapter 7. Solomon had just finished building the Temple – everything he had planned to do he had 'successfully completed'. That same night the Lord appeared to Solomon and confirmed that he accepted the Temple, and went on to tell him that in times of drought or pestilence, if the people humbled themselves and prayed, then he would hear from heaven, forgive their sin and heal their land (verse 14). There is mutual giving and receiving – 'If my people pray. . . then I will . . .' It is a basic biblical principle that God moves when people pray. That is why quiet times are so important. It is through them, and especially through our prayers, that we bring God into human situations and circumstances. It is through our quiet times that we get to know the Lord in a deeper way and are then in a position to give to him as well as receiving from him.

Accepting God's invitation is just the first step in God's plan for our involvement in the salvation of mankind, as well as for our own spiritual growth. When we realise how much God desires our company, then we will be well on the way to gaining a totally different outlook on this important subject.

PRACTICAL

Decide right now that you will respond to God's invitation and spend time with him daily. Let the following prayer be your response to God's RSVP.

PRAYER

Father, I thank you that you call me by name to come into your presence, and for showing me how important it is for my spiritual growth. I thank you for loving me and creating me for your glory, and I accept your invitation to spend time with you each day.   Amen.

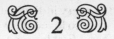

2

The Aims and Benefits of a Quiet Time

There is no doubt that the Christian who neglects a regular meeting with God will have only a lukewarm experience of him, resulting inevitably in a weak and ineffective Christian witness. Not only that; the Lord has countless benefits and blessings to give to his children, but again, how can he do so if we do not accept his invitation and keep our daily appointment with him? God longs for us to spend time with him each day so that he can pass his blessings on to us face to face – just as it is so much nicer for us to give a present to somebody in person rather than send it through the post. My mother now lives in Spain, and on a visit to her I realised how expensive it was to buy clothes out there, and how depleted her wardrobe had become. I therefore took great delight in buying a couple of dresses and sending them out to her via a relative going on holiday. But I would much rather have given them to her personally and seen her delight and pleasure.

So what are the blessings we can receive from a personal, regular encounter with God? For a start, we will know his love and acceptance. 'No longer do I call you servants, but friends,' says Jesus in John 15.15. Jesus changes our status, and accepts us as equals. Not only that, but we are also described as children of God and heirs – joint beneficiaries with Christ (Romans 8.17). This is gloriously reaffirmed in the first chapter of Ephesians, where Paul tells his readers that we are all partakers of Christ's inheritance – so that whatever God passes on to his Son in his 'will', also passes to us as joint heirs with Christ.

9

The deepest need of every individual is to be loved. That need is met in God, who 'so loved the world that he gave his Son' (John 3.16). When I first became a Christian, the lady who counselled me told me to put my own name in that verse: 'For God so loved Jean, that he gave his only begotten Son, that if Jean believes in him she should not perish but have eternal life.' That made the transaction so much more personal! The reason why I need to be loved is because I was created in the image of God (Genesis 1.26), and we are told in 1 John 4.8 that 'God is Love.' Therefore I have inherited the need to be loved and the capacity to love from God, and these longings are satisfied as I spend time with him.

Another benefit we receive from spending time with God is guidance for each day and for our future. It is very easy to fall into the habit of forgetting to ask God such basic questions as: 'What do *you* want me to do with my life?', or 'What shall I do today?', or 'Is this the person you want me to marry?' As long ago as 1714, Matthew Henry, a Presbyterian minister who wrote a commentary on the Bible that is still widely used today, wrote on this subject: 'Do we not know that we have daily work to do for God, and have we not then business with God to beg of him to show us what he would have us do, to direct us in it, and strengthen us for it? To seek to him for assistance and acceptance, that he will work in us both to will and to do that which is good.'[1]

As the pace of life speeds up, it is more important than ever that Christians find peace and refreshment and receive strength to carry on. A marvellous description of the antidote to a tired and weary Christian is found in Acts 3.19, where Peter says: 'Times of refreshing come from the presence of the Lord.' If we are tired, weary or fed up, the last thing we may feel like doing is having a quiet time. Yet the Bible says that it is those who wait on the Lord who find that their strength is renewed, and they are given the power to run and not be weary, to walk and not faint (Isaiah 40.31). Martin Luther is reported to have said: 'If I fail to

10

spend two hours in prayer each morning the devil gets the victory through the day. I have so much business I cannot get on without spending three hours daily in prayer.'[2]

An inevitable result of having a regular devotional time will be the changes that take place in us as we grow as Christians, and this ties in with the aim that God has in mind when he calls us to spend time with him. His aim is that we should become more like his Son, Jesus. He 'predestined us to be conformed to the image of his son' (Romans 8.29). This passage goes on to explain that Jesus is the first of many brethren, the first of many others, who will be called 'Christians', or 'like Christ' in the world. It is only as we spend time with God that changes begin to take place in our lives, and over the months and years we do indeed find ourselves altering, and our personalities becoming more like the Lord Jesus.

One of my favourite Bible verses is 2 Corinthians 3.17: 'We all, with unveiled face, beholding the glory of the Lord, are being changed into his likeness from one degree of glory to another.' I used to read that verse over and over to myself and took great joy and delight in it, and couldn't stop sharing it with my friends. It became even more precious when I discovered from the notes in the margin of my Bible that 'beholding' also means 'reflecting', and I began to see that as we spend time with the Lord, as we look at Jesus, so we reflect his glory, his image, his life, his nature and his personality into our very selves, until we become like him. Just as we look in a mirror and see a reflection of our own faces, so in our quiet times we look at Jesus and begin to see him reflected in our lives.

We see this in the story of Moses, when he had been up on the mountain to spend time with God. When he returned from the mountain his face shone so much that he had to put a veil over it. Moses didn't realise at first that the skin of his face was shining because he had been talking with God (Exodus 34.29–35). I can remember being told a similar story when I was at a Girls Brigade camp in my early teens. It concerned a young woman whose face really did shine with the inner light of the Lord. When this was pointed out to her she looked in a mirror to see for herself, but of course she couldn't see anything unusual or different! It is other people who will see the reflected glory of the Lord shining in our faces and in our lives.

God has yet another aim in mind as we spend time with him, and that is the union of our spirits with his Holy Spirit. 'He who is united to the Lord becomes one spirit with him' (1 Corinthians 6.17). These words need to be repeated over and over again until the truth of them sinks in. We are told to worship God in spirit and in truth (John 4.24), and this is now possible through the ministry of the Holy Spirit.[3] God says 'I will put my Spirit within you' (Ezekiel 36). When we really believe this promise and experience it, we will be able to relax into worshipping God 'in the Spirit'.

We are made up of body, soul and spirit. Through our bodies we are aware of the world around us, through our souls we have self consciousness, and through our spirits we have awareness of God. The soul is the meeting place, the point of union, between body and spirit. Through the body we relate to the world around us through our five senses, and through our spirits we relate to the spiritual world. But too often our souls tend to be far more conscious of the physical world than of the spiritual one. Because of sin, our spirit, that part created to be in contact with God in the spiritual realm, then goes into decline and becomes dormant. When we meet with the Lord at our conversion, or seek to renew and deepen our faith, he puts his Spirit upon us and our spirits are rekindled, and then our souls and bodies are restored to their rightful relationship with the Father. 'He restores my soul', says the Psalmist in Psalm 23.3. We have now entered a new three-dimensional life. Before, we were living only through our souls and bodies in this material world – now we are in touch with the heavenlies – the spiritual realm. Our quiet times are necess-

12

ary to keep that vital channel open between our spirits and the Holy Spirit.

If the Holy Spirit is active in our lives, it follows that there will have to be changes. If we desire to grow more like Christ we cannot expect to stay exactly the same people. Paul, in his letter to the Philippians, says, 'Work out your own salvation with fear and trembling.' This may seem difficult to understand at first, but over the years I have come to appreciate a little of Paul's meaning. When we initially come to the Lord we are concerned with the salvation of our souls and entry into heaven; but as we learn more in the Christian life we will realise that there are many areas in our lives that need saving. Yes, of course these areas were covered and 'saved' the day we accepted Christ, but very often we need to work through with the Lord his salvation in these new areas.

For instance, when I became a Christian, I had no knowledge or experience of what is now called 'healing of the memories' – the power of God to sort out negative experiences in our past that have hindered us spiritually or emotionally.[4] It was not until fifteen years later that a need arose in my life, and I was able to 'work out my own salvation' in an area that needed the ministry of the Cross, in a way that was relevant and that had my full consent and knowledge. This need involved the teenage memories I had of my father, which were rather painful. Much as I loved him at the time, I realise looking back that he found it difficult to give or receive love, and eventually my mother and I left our lovely home to live in a bed-sitter together. By this time I was working, and engaged to be married, but leaving home in such circumstances was still a painful process.

During a time of depression many years later, I felt the Lord pin-pointing this area in my life, and showing me that I had never forgiven my father and that I still harboured bitterness, resentment and even some hatred towards him. During lunch time one day, Peter and I sat down to talk and pray through this problem. I confessed my wrong attitude and through prayer forgave my father and released him from all my wrong emotions. In my mind's eye I pictured myself hugging and kissing him and our relationship being restored. The truly amazing point of my healing of these painful memories was the fact that this restoration took place about nine months after my father's death. During this time I experienced three dreams which very specifically confirmed to me that what had taken place through prayer for healing of the memories, also took place in the spiritual realm. I discovered, too, that God, who is Lord of time, is able to take us back to any time in our past and will heal anything that hinders our development as healthy, well adjusted, Spirit-filled Christians. Once this healing of my memories, mind and emotions had taken place, I began to see a real improvement in my physical health, and look back on that time as a major step in the healing of my depression.

As we spend time with God over the months and years we will find him putting his finger on wrong thoughts, habits, relationships, hurtful memories or traumatic happenings in our past. We can then take each exposed and painful spot back to the Cross, and as we confess and forgive, so God works his work of salvation in these new areas, bringing restoration and healing. This can be done either on our own, or through the prayerful help of close friends. Either way, we can be sure that the Lord restores the years that the locust has eaten (Joel 2.25).

So we can see that, while we may come to God to give him our praise and worship, and in turn to receive many blessings and benefits, this is also a time for God to fulfill his purposes in our lives, to unite our spirits with his Holy Spirit, and to make us more like his son, Jesus.

PRACTICAL

1 Look up again in the Bible the things that we receive from God and try to discover more and add them to the list.

14

2   Study Romans chapter 8 for the outworking of the Spirit in our lives.
3   Prayerfully ask the Lord to show you areas in your life that need healing and restoring.

PRAYER

Thank you, Father, that I receive so many benefits when I come into your presence, and that you are willing to shower me with so much goodness and blessing. Thank you even more, Lord, that your ideals for me are so much higher than mine, and that your desire for me is that I become like your Son, the Lord Jesus Christ. I dare to ask you to change me, and to work in areas of my life that need your saving touch.   Amen.

NOTES

1   Matthew Henry, *Directions for Daily Communion with God* (Evangelical Press).
2   Quoted in E.M. Bounds, *Power through Prayer* (Baker Book House).
3   For the work of the Holy Spirit see chapter 8.
4   Most, if not all, of us have been hurt emotionally at one time or another. When praying with people for healing of the memories, they are gently taken back to the time when they were hurt, asked to picture the scene in their minds and to describe it, but this time to visualise the presence of Jesus with them. When we add the visible presence of the Lord in traumatic and hurtful memories, the situation is wonderfully changed and the person is set free to live fully in the present. For a detailed book on the subject, read *Emotionally Free*, by Rita Bennett (Kingsway).

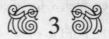

When and Where

Once we are really serious about spending a part of each day alone with the Lord, then the obvious thing to do is to ask him to show us when we are to do it.

When I first thought to ask God this most practical of questions, I found he was ready and able to give me suggestions. God is fully aware of our crowded schedules, and well able to show us how to fit such a time in. For instance, like most mothers, I allowed my two-and-a-half-year-old daughter to watch *Playschool* on the television each morning. While she was doing so, I used to hurry round the house, hoovering, polishing, ironing or cooking. Then one day it suddenly dawned on me that instead of selfishly using that half an hour to do what I wanted (or at least what I thought ought to be done) here was the ideal opportunity to spend the time meeting with the Lord. I realised that the Lord had put this idea into my mind, so I began to try his suggestion. After settling my daughter down in front of her favourite programme with a drink and a biscuit, I would slip into another room to have my quiet time. It worked very well, except for the occasional interruption like: 'Please, Mummy, can you take me to the toilet', or 'I've spilt my drink on the carpet.' As she got older she began to realise what I was doing and would say, 'Are you going to talk to Jesus now?' She even asked that same question two or three years later when she saw me standing in the doorway with my Bible in my hands! Even though I had only twenty or twenty-five minutes, I found that the Lord graciously allowed me into his presence very quickly, so that I was able to make full use of the time available.

Once my youngest daughter started at a playgroup, I had two whole mornings a week to myself – bliss after having children at home for many years! I felt it right to increase my quiet times to an hour, even though it was rather a sacrifice to begin with. However, I soon found any such sacrifice on my part was amply rewarded by the Lord in blessings, and an increased awareness of his presence. I began to see, too, that God is Lord of time, and my housework and other duties seemed to get done much more quickly and efficiently once I had a regular meeting with him.

Of course, I am sharing my own personal experience as a housewife and mother. You may be at work or at school, and have other difficulties to overcome in the matter of finding time. When I was at work I sometimes spent my lunch hour in a church near my office; it was bliss to enter the quiet and tranquillity after a hectic morning typing, filing and answering the phone. For those at school or college, the pressures of studies may seem more important than meeting with God, but here again, the Lord is able to make us more efficient if we put him first. Indeed, it is idolatory to put anything else before God. A divorced friend shared with me how she had early morning quiet times, which were a great strength and blessing. When her son started school she was able to have one during the day. Now she is working full time, and finds weekends and school holidays are the occasions when she can spend more time with the Lord.

Thinking about this subject, I was reminded of the manna in the Old Testament. It was there in the morning, ready to be picked up by the people of Israel, but by midday the sun had melted it away. The Israelites had to pick up the manna each day – they were not to leave some for the following morning. Those who disobeyed God and kept some found that 'it bred worms and stank' (Exodus

16.4). The only day they could gather a double portion was the sixth day so that they need do no work by gathering the manna on the following day of rest. This reminds us that we need to come to the Lord daily for our spiritual food, and should not try to carry over one day's blessings into the next.

When people in the Bible felt led to perform some sacred act, it was often very early in the morning that they did so. Jacob rose early after his dream of angels ascending and descending the ladder (Genesis 28.18). Gideon would not have had his experience with the fleece if he had not been willing to get up while the dew was still around (Judges 6.38). Samuel (1 Samuel 9.26) and David (1 Samuel 17.20) were also early risers. Of course, Jesus himself set us the supreme example by rising 'a great while before day', in order to pray (Mark 1.35). So the scriptural pattern and ideal seems to be to start early, not least so that we can receive the Lord's guidance and protection for the coming hours. Besides, most of us are much fresher first thing in the morning, and it hardly seems right to come to the Lord when we are tired and jaded by the day's business.

It is clear that, when we are really determined to have a quiet time with the Lord, we shall find that there have to be changes in our life patterns, and these may well include getting up earlier. A friend of mine bought herself a bedside lamp so that she could read and pray first thing in the morning – though I find personally that it is far better to get up, wash and dress before meeting the Lord. If mornings are difficult for you, you could have just five or ten minutes saying 'Good morning' to God before you go out, thanking him for his protection during the night, and asking for his guidance during the day. You could then find a quiet room during your lunch break (or a church, as I did) where you can spend a longer time in praise and worship, study and prayer.

An idea for those at home is to share housework or child-minding with a close friend, so that you can take turns in having a morning or afternoon free for your devotions. You may need to do your cooking at different times, or organise your meals in such a way that the best part of the day is reserved for God – in fact, planning a week's or a month's menus in advance greatly reduces the amount of time wasted in wondering, 'What shall we have for tea tonight?'

Though I felt that God had solved my mid-week problems, weekends still were not adequately provided for, so instead of doing the weekend cake-baking on a Saturday morning, I found that I could sometimes fit it in while preparing Friday evening's meal. Whatever your circumstances, finding time for God is mainly a question of thinking ahead and being well organised.

If you are married, with children, then the situation needs to be talked over with your partner, so that you can agree to take it in turns to look after the children while the other partner has a quiet time.

We also have to learn to be realistic about our human frailties. In the winter, I tried 'listening' to the Lord a couple of times directly after lunch and in front of the fire. The inevitable happened and I fell asleep!

There will, however, be occasions when genuine problems will hinder our quiet times. Such hindrances can include ill health, pregnancy, a new baby, a recent bereavement, depression, shift-work or moving house. Any of these can stop us finding time for the Lord, or can dampen our enthusiasm. If there are genuine reasons for not making ourselves available to God on a few occasions, we should not worry unduly, or feel excessively guilty. But if, on the other hand, our lapses are due to wrong priorities or laziness, then obviously we need to sort the situation out. So, what can we do when we are unable to have a regular quiet time for a while?

First of all it helps to remember that God understands, and is still beside us and with us. If we have been in the habit of having a daily devotional time, then we shall already have achieved a sense of the Lord's presence and a good knowledge of Scripture, and we can draw on this and on the fact that Jesus covers us with his love. But we can also seek covering of another sort.

When my husband gave me my wedding ring on the day we were married, it delighted me to discover that he had had this verse inscribed on the inside: 'If one is down the other will lift him up' (see Ecclesiastes 4.10). Over the years I have found that it is Peter who has been the one to lift me up when I am down spiritually, or for one reason or another unable to pray or worship or study the Bible. During times of ill health, pregnancy, or when for other reasons it was difficult to meet with God regularly, he has been the one to cover me with his prayers. In fact this is part of a husband's role as head of the wife, in loving and caring for her and presenting her beautiful before God in the same way that Christ presents the Church to God (Ephesians 5).

I once spent a whole week when I felt I was unable to enter the Lord's presence, no matter how hard I tried. By the Saturday I was in tears, and Peter found me crying in the lounge. When I told him how I was feeling, he sent me up to our bedroom with the cassette recorder and a tape of Christian songs and told me to praise the Lord. I protested that I didn't feel like it, but he gently encouraged me, so I obediently traipsed upstairs and spent twenty minutes or so trying to join in with the praise tape. I began very squeakily but gradually was able to sing more meaningfully. Within a few days I was back to my usual close relationship with the Lord; but it took the covering and lifting up of my husband to persuade me to do what I was unable to do for myself.

We all need to be surrounded in love and prayer by someone, and if you are married then your partner can do this for you. If you are not married, or your husband or wife is not a Christian, then you can seek out a close friend and agree to be honest with each other and share when you need covering or lifting. This may be difficult at first, as none of us likes to admit that things are wrong, or that we can't cope. But we shall find that just sharing any problem is a relief, as well as knowing we can get such help from sharing and receiving this special kind of love.

A dear friend had recently lost her husband, and though up to that point her quiet times had been very precious to her, she found directly after her husband's death that she was completely unable to pray. She would sit in the Lord's presence, but all the words were gone. She was wisely advised by the vicar just to rest in her Saviour, as he certainly understood how she felt; and in the meantime she relied on the prayers of others in the church fellowship to cover herself and her family.[1]

In practical terms, what can the one who covers actually do for us? Like my husband, they can encourage and help us out of any difficult situations. They can be a listening ear, which is one of the most valuable ministries which anyone can have. They can, most importantly, pray for us and with us. If it is a long term situation, like the first weeks with a new baby or a bout of illness, they can share the fruits of their own quiet times with us, talking about the Lord and passing on to us the things they have learned in prayer and study.

If we genuinely have no time to sit down with the Lord, that fact alone need not stop our experiencing his presence. If we have a cassette recorder we can play Christian song and music tapes during the day; this is a marvellous lifter of spirits. Or we can listen to teaching tapes, which will keep us fed spiritually, while we do the household chores, feed the baby or drive to work. If we have memorised verses of Scripture we can meditate on them in coffee breaks, on the train, in the bus queue or in the supermarket. It is a simple thing to write out some Bible verses and have them in front of us at the kitchen sink, or by our bed, or in the car. I have a card pinned up on the sloping ceiling of our attic bedroom just above my bed, with a description of the armour of God (Ephesians 6) written out in large print. It reminds me to put on the armour each day for my protection and covering.

There are so many things we can do to 'keep the Lord always before us' (Psalm 16.8), and by following them, and if possible making sure we are blanketed in prayer by another caring Christian, we can keep our desire for fellowship with the Lord strong and fresh.

Having decided on the best time for you personally to meet with God, the next question is, where? Like me, you may find that the place varies, perhaps according to the seasons. During the summer I like to go into our lounge at the back of the house. It is the room where we have met as a house group for many years, and I feel that even the walls are impregnated with the peace and presence of the Lord – the way some old churches feel when we enter them. In the winter I mostly use another room where it is warmer. The important thing is to remember the words of Jesus himself: 'When you pray, go into your room and shut the door and pray to your Father who is in secret; and your Father who sees in secret will reward you' (Matthew 6.6). I like the Authorised Version of this verse, for it adds the word 'openly' at the end. In other words, I may spend my time alone with the Lord in such a way that it is a secret between him and me, but the rewards and blessings he gives me will be evident for all to see.

Whatever place you choose, at whatever time, it is important to be on your own with the Lord. You cannot easily have a meaningful relationship with him if there are others in the room. You will certainly be greatly hindered from worshipping, singing and praying if that is the case. Husbands and wives may like to have a prayer time together – in fact it is lovely when they do – but they also each need a time for private devotions.

Looking again at the words of Jesus in Matthew 6, we see that our Lord takes it for granted that we will pray. He does not say 'if you pray', but 'when you pray'. So the Lord is expecting us to set time aside to be with him; let us make every effort to fulfill his expectations!

PRACTICAL

1 Sort out your day into time segments, e.g. 7–8 hours for sleep, 6–7 hours at work, 1–2 hours travelling, 1–2 hours eating, etc. See where in your busy day you can fit in time for the Lord. Bearing in mind that 'the earlier the better', you may need to examine the last hours of the day to see if you are going to bed too late, or watching too much television, which stops you waking early the following morning. Do this prayerfully, asking the Lord for his advice and suggestions.

2 Ask the Lord to show you someone who will be prepared to cover you in prayer as you in turn cover them.

PRAYER

Lord, I do sincerely desire to spend more time with you. I confess it is my own lack of desire and laziness that have stopped me in the past. I pray that you will thrill me again with the joy of your presence, and show me when it is best for me to meet with you each day. Amen.

NOTE

1 For more about covering, see Jean Brand, *A Woman's Privilege* (Christian Woman Books, Triangle), especially chapter 7.

4

The Tools Required

If we want to take our daily meeting with God seriously, then we shall need to prepare ourselves properly and have the right tools available as we come into his presence. My mother always taught me when cooking to get everything I would need out ready beforehand: it's so annoying having to look through the kitchen drawers for the rolling pin if your hands are covered in flour! Similarly, if the Lord is in the middle of speaking to us, or giving us the words of a prophecy[1], we can hardly rush out of the room to hunt for pencil and paper – so it is important to have several things by us when we sit down to meet with him.

The first priority, of course, is your Bible. As we read and study the Scriptures, God ensures that his word sinks deep into our very being. The word of God is extremely powerful, but we need to take it into our minds and hearts for it to become effective. It is helpful to have one or two different translations beside us, especially if we are doing some 'in depth' study. As we compare translations we can be surprised at the nuances of meaning that appear, and we can get a more rounded understanding of a particular verse or passage. You will find a wide choice of Bibles available at your local Christian bookshop, and the assistants there will be able to advise you on the version that will suit your needs best. Try to buy a well-bound edition – you will be using it regularly and a paperback version will not stand up to such frequent use. You may also find it helpful to choose a Bible with chain references. This means that if a verse seems important to you as you read it, and you want to

24

study it further, the reference in the margin in the middle of the page will tell you of other verses with a similar meaning or subject. In this way you can check many passages one against the other, forwards and backwards in the Bible.

The second tool necessary is a pen or pencil. I find it practically impossible to read Scripture without a pen or pencil in my hand to underline verses and make notes. Some people have special methods for doing this, perhaps using one colour to mark passages referring to salvation, another for the Holy Spirit, a third for promises and so on. Special soft crayons and fluorescent markers are available for use on the thin paper of Bibles. Other people simply underline a verse or passage as they feel the Lord speaking to them through it, or make brief notes on it.

This leads on to the third item that is necessary – paper. This could be a notebook, a card index filing box, or a large folder of notepaper. Because our quiet times give God the opportunity to speak to us, it is important that we write down the things he says. We also need to keep a note of the thoughts and ideas that come to us as we read and study the Scriptures. My own quiet times became far more personal and meaningful when I began keeping notes and writing things down. I first of all used an old card index box which I found in our attic while rummaging around one day. I had diligently used it when I first purchased my freezer, but the enthusiasm for methodically keeping records soon wore off, and there were still plenty of blank cards. Each day as I read and studied a passage of the Bible I would use a new card to write down any thoughts and ideas that came to me, checking cross references and making various other notes. As I gained more eagerness and joy in studying I soon had to buy new cards, and now I have quite a collection of notes on the things the Lord has shown me. When he brings a special verse alive to me I keep a note of it on a separate card, together with the circumstances of the day and a note of my feelings at the time.

I also find it beneficial to keep a note of my prayers, not

neglecting a record of how and when God answered. I found doing this was a great boost to my faith, for it enabled me to see the way the Lord was working in people's lives, and to thank him accordingly. A prayer list also keeps us on our toes in praying regularly for people, and stops us forgetting to pray. The list should be flexible, so that you can add to it easily.

I have also found it useful to keep a note of comments and ideas from other Christian writers, from the books or articles that I read. The late Catherine Marshall wrote copious notes all her life, and we should certainly be the poorer if she had not done so; her books are full of the Lord's dealings with her, and very valuable and edifying for us. In the foreword to her last book, *Meeting God at every Turn*, she describes how she hunted through her written records going back over forty years, contained in letters, books, scrapbooks and diaries. Out of all this treasure came a total of sixteen books, all of which have helped and inspired thousands of Christians all over the world.

Another area I keep notes on during my quiet times is the way the Lord is dealing with me personally, and with my family. When we write down our thoughts and attitudes over some sin or temptation it puts things into perspective and helps to clarify the situation. Keeping a note of how we coped during a particular crisis, and how the Lord worked to help us, can encourage us for future occasions. Again, it provides more evidence for which to thank and praise him.

This practice proved vital for me during a time when I lost my wedding and engagement rings. I had taken them off while I rubbed in some hand cream, and a short while later they had disappeared. We had several children in our house that day, and we realised that one of them had probably taken the rings, but after carefully and gently questioning each child we were no nearer discovering the whereabouts of the jewellery. After the children had gone home, I spent the rest of the day searching through every room in the house, gradually getting more and more upset.

Over the course of the next few weeks the Lord dealt with me in several different stages. First of all, I had to be willing to accept that my rings might be lost for ever. This was, of course, very hard, but the Lord led me to pray the prayer of relinquishment, in which I willingly handed them over to him for him to do with as he willed. It was a real time of testing. As each day went by, I wrote down the events, prayers, thoughts and messages from close friends, and these were a great comfort to me.

During this time the Lord also showed me that I had to forgive the child who I thought might have taken the rings; and not just to forgive him, but to go on to actively bless, love and support him in prayer. A friend shared with me that after she had prayed she felt the Lord telling her that the child had problems at school, so we concentrated on praying for him in that environment, and that any pressures there would be released.

Three weeks later the rings were found by the child's mother. I, of course, felt just like the woman in the parable who had lost her coin, and when she found it she called together her friends and neighbours saying: 'Rejoice with me, for I have found the coin which I had lost' (Luke 15.8.9). Now I can look back on the things I wrote down during that time, and really praise the Lord for the way he worked in my life. If I had not kept notes at the time, though, I'm sure I would have forgotten some of the relevant points. The Lord always brings good out of bad if we let him work in his way, and the child concerned and I now have a new understanding and love for each other.

When Peter and I led a course on Quiet Times in our church, we initially bought twenty little notebooks to hand out to those who came. We encouraged them to use their notebooks, and shared with them the sort of things we wrote down, and the blessings and advantages that resulted. Now many of these folk have gone on to using notebooks regularly as part of their quiet times. One young woman testifies that they make a major contribution to her

27

Christian experience. She is at present keeping meticulous details of the way the Lord is working in her life as she and another pray for the physical healing of her body, damaged through polio.

Along with your Bible, it is helpful to have a concordance. Your own Bible may well have one at the back, or you can buy them separately. A concordance removes a lot of the hard work of Bible study. For example, if you wish to study verses on faith, the concordance, depending on its size, will list most, or all, of the verses that quote that word.

One year when Peter was teaching at a summer school in Canada, we lived on campus in accommodation that was looked after by a nun, with whom we became close friends during our stay. We enjoyed sharing prayer and Bible study with her and the other sisters. During a time of discussion one evening, a Bible verse was mentioned, but nobody could remember where it came from. When we got back to our room it took us only a minute or so to locate it in the concordance at the back of our Bible. One nun was most surprised when we showed her the reference the next day – I think she had visions of us wading through the Bible all night long! She was delighted when we explained to her the mysteries of the concordance, and it opened up for her a whole new area of Bible study.

Another useful aid as we study Scripture is a Bible dictionary, which, like an ordinary one, gives the meaning of the words used in Scripture. This is really helpful when we are studying, and can add a great deal to our overall understanding of God's word. There are also plenty of books available which expound, or make clearer, the Scriptures, and books that deal with the archaeological, social and historical aspects of God's word. Bible handbooks and commentaries help to clarify or expand ideas that we meet in the Bible, and there are many sorts of Bible study notes, intended for daily use and aimed at Christians of different ages and at different stages in the Christian life. These include *Every Day with Jesus*, and Scripture Union notes, and can be bought at any Christian book shop.

If you look round your local Christian book shop you will also find many other devotional and inspirational books. *Daily Light* has been a firm favourite with many Christians over the years; it consists of verses of Scripture, collected together under a given theme, for every day of the year, morning and evening, and can be obtained in several different Bible versions. Books such as this can contribute greatly to our time with the Lord.

There is one more tool we can bring as we come into the Lord's presence, and that is music. It doesn't matter whether we are musical or not, nor whether we sing well or badly – the Lord loves to hear us praise him in song. The Authorised Version of Psalm 22.3 says that the Lord 'inhabits the praises of Israel', which gives us a lovely picture of him actually dwelling in the praises we bring him. As we sing and praise and worship, therefore, either using a song book or singing from memory, we are declaring to all the heavenly hosts around us that the Lord is dwelling with us and in us. The subject of music and singing forms such an important part of our quiet time that it is dealt with more fully in chapter 9. Hymns can also be used as devotional readings, either quietly or out loud.

Having gathered together the tools of our Christian trade, we then need to prepare our homes and our environment. It is important to create an atmosphere in our homes that is conducive to prayer and praise, worship and study, and that means taking stock of what we see and hear. Remember the old Sunday School hymn? 'O be careful little eyes what you see, and be careful little ears what you hear, for the Father up above is looking down in love, so be careful little eyes what you see.' If we take a good look at our homes with the eyes of Christ we may have to remove pictures, art objects, books or records that are in any way alien to the presence of God's Spirit.

Many years ago Peter brought an Aztec calendar home

from the States. It was large and round with a bronze finish and looked really nice hanging on the wall in our lounge. As we grew closer to the Lord, however, we began to realise that the message it portrayed and the culture it represented was alien to the Christian principles we wanted to have in our home. So one afternoon Peter took it down to the end of the garden and broke it up. Some novels on an occult theme were thrown on the bonfire, for anything connected with witch-craft or the occult can have a subtle but harmful influence over our homes and lives. Likewise, records and tapes need carefully sorting through. Jamie Buckingham has a powerful chapter in his book *Risky Living* on the influence of certain pop and heavy beat records, and a hair-raising story concerning a particular record album his son had purchased.[2]

The television is probably another area where we may have to stand firm and say 'no' despite the children's cries of protest. I found a verse in the Psalms recently that could be readily applied to this area: 'I will not set before my eyes anything that is base' (Psalm 101.3). Weeks later I looked at that verse again and noticed for the first time that the words immediately preceding were: 'I will walk with integrity of heart within my house.' These verses speak eloquently of how we should behave in our own homes, and the standards we should seek to keep.

We are not being asked to do anything that others have not already done, for several passages in the Old Testament tell of people being told to throw out of their homes the idols belonging to other religions, or anything that would take the place of God in their lives (e.g. 2 Chronicles 15.8).

Another area I personally had to consider was the radio. Much as I liked to listen to the news first thing in the morning while preparing breakfast, I found the noise and discordant voices jarred on the atmosphere round the breakfast table, and the children's voices seemed to rise higher and louder to counteract that of the newscaster. So I now try to make sure that the radio is turned off and that there is peace and quiet while we are eating. There is so much noise in our lives today that it requires positive action to work at creating an atmosphere of peace.

Apart from removing offending items from our homes, we can be far more positive, by replacing them with things that are honest, just, lovely and true (Philippians 4.8). One way of doing this is to play quietly one of the many praise and worship tapes or records now available, to create the right atmosphere for ourselves and especially for our children. One morning I left my eldest daughter in charge of the younger children while I drove Peter to the station. On my return I was surprised and delighted to find them sitting round the table eating their breakfast with a praise tape playing quietly in the background.

There are also many lovely posters and pictures to be bought from Christian book shops to brighten our homes, as well as hundreds of good books, fiction and non-fiction, to fill our bookshelves. In today's modern society, when more and more people have videos in their homes, we can obtain plenty of good Christian video films to show to family, friends and neighbours. One of the young men in our church is gradually collecting a number of videos from Christian distributors and invites friends and neighbours in to see them.

Preparing our homes in this way, and collecting together the right tools, is one of the ways we can show the Lord we are really serious about living his life in today's world.

Once we have prepared our homes and ourselves, we shall begin to sense a growing feeling of excitement and expectancy as we enter into the very presence of God himself.

PRACTICAL

1   Buy a good-sized notebook and place it ready with a pen or pencil, together with your Bible and other 'tools'.

2 Prayerfully, with the Lord, check over each room of your home, and all your books, records, tapes etc. Remove and throw away any that the Lord shows you may be having a harmful influence on your home and family.

3 Do a study on idols – check in your concordance for various verses, and follow them through in your Bible chain reference system.

PRAYER

Father, thank you that by providing myself with the tools of my Christian trade I am also showing you that I want to work with you in becoming more like Jesus, and in passing on your message of salvation to a needy world. Help me to prepare my home to be a fit place for you to live in, and to make sure that nothing stands between me and you.

Amen.

SOME CHRISTIAN VIDEO DISTRIBUTORS

Bagster Video, Westbrook House, 76 High Street, Alton, Hants.
Christian Video Experience, 6 Cecil Way, Hayes, Bromley, Kent.
Christian Video Library, 12 Oxleay Road, Harrow, Middx.
CTVC Beeson's Yard, Bury Lane, Rickmansworth, Herts.
Harvestime Video Library, Harvestime House, 136 Hall Lane, Bradford, West Yorks.
Kingsway Video, Lottbridge Drove, Eastbourne, East Sussex.
International Films, 235 Shaftesbury Avenue, London WC2H 8EL.
Scripture Union, 130 City Road, London EC1V 2NJ.
Signpost Christian Video Centre, Westway, Ruislip, Middx.

NOTES

1 For prophecy, see chapter 14.
2 Jamie Buckingham, *Risky Living* (Kingsway).

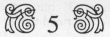

Preparing Ourselves

Although we have a personal invitation to enter the holy of holies, to meet with our great and wonderful Lord, we must beware of barging in to his presence without due thought or reverence or without any preparation. Recently my aunt and uncle had the privilege of going to a garden party at Buckingham Palace. It goes without saying that they took a great deal of care in their preparation, making sure they were clean and tidy, had carefully chosen new clothes, and were on their best behaviour. Of course, we know that we have access at any time to the throne room of the King of kings, and that our acceptance does not depend on any special effort on our part. Nevertheless, because we love and honour him, we will wish to make some personal preparation before we draw near with confidence to the throne of grace (Hebrews 4.16).

The first element of preparation I would suggest is faith. The great chapter on this subject, Hebrews 11, lists men and women who lived and died in faith throughout the history of the Israelites. Faith, says the writer of Hebrews, is believing something we cannot actually see. We have already exercised this faculty by accepting the Lord Jesus as our saviour, and believing that his Spirit has come to live with us. The key verse for us is Hebrews 11.6: 'Without faith it is impossible to please him, for whoever would draw near to God must believe that he exists, and that he rewards those who seek him.'

Unless we actually believe that God is waiting for us when we begin our devotions, the whole thing will be a waste of time and effort. Of course, the more often we meet God in this way, the less need there will be for this initial preparation. The more we read the Bible and spend time with God, the more our faith will grow.

There are, however, times when our feelings keep us from believing that the Lord is present. Although we aim to experience the presence of the Lord every time as we wait upon him, it is important not to fall into the trap of relying on our feelings. It may sometimes just be a case of gritting our teeth and accepting with our will that if God says he will meet with us – then he will certainly keep his promise.

The second step in preparation is confession. The Psalmist recognised that 'if I had cherished iniquity in my heart, the Lord would not have listened' (Psalm 66.18). In other words – sin is a block. It actually stops God from hearing us, so if we are knowingly being sinful in some area of our lives there is little point in setting aside part of the day to be with him, to worship, or even to pray, for our prayers just will not reach him. Not that he cannot *hear* us; but just as a loving human parent may refuse to answer a disobedient child, so if sin is blocking the way, he will not *listen*. Perhaps that is why we sometimes feel that our prayers are just hitting the ceiling and fail to reach God's heart!

However, the Bible has shown us the remedy: 'I acknowledged my sin to thee, and I did not hide my iniquity; I said, "I will confess my transgressions to the Lord"; then thou didst forgive the guilt of my sin' (Psalm 32.5). When we confess our sins to the Lord the blockage is removed and the channel is clear again. We are then 'righteous', and can enjoy an unbroken relationship with God. We are made right with God, not by any works of our own, but purely by the blood of Christ, and so our prayers will now be effective and powerful (James 5.16).

Over the years my confessions have usually been pretty general, but one day I was conscious of some attitudes and thoughts and resentments that were very heavy on my heart when I woke up, and I couldn't wait till the children had gone to school before I had the chance of confessing them fully to the Lord and offloading the weight of sin. As I meditated and confessed, the Lord led me to Psalm 51.6: 'Behold, thou desirest truth in the inward being; therefore teach me wisdom in my secret heart.' God knows us through and through, and all our sins – big or little – are exposed to his all-searching eye. But he also wants us to be truthful with ourselves and to admit just what we are like. By examining our daily lives (the thoughts, words and deeds that may be hurtful to us and harmful to others), we can see what our faults are and try to do something about them. After reading that verse from the Psalms, I faced up to myself and confessed my sin to the Lord. Then I experienced the truth of the words of Scripture, that 'If we confess our sins, he is faithful and just, and will forgive our sins and cleanse us from all unrighteousness' (1 John 1.9). For me it felt as if a great load had been lifted off my shoulders.

When I confessed to the Lord that particular morning, I found it especially helpful to do so out loud. A few minutes later I discovered that writing it down was yet another step to make the process of confession more meaningful. As I began to put all my bad thoughts down on paper I experienced real release and blessing. They looked so horrible written down, too! After this exercise I was on the point of tearing it up as a sign to me of God's forgiveness, but on reflection I decided to keep that particular card by way of a reminder of the power of confession and the joy of being forgiven.

Another way of acknowledging our sin is to confess to another Christian, for we are told to 'confess your sins to one another and pray for one another' (James 5.16). When we are truly sorry, and brave enough to confess to another person, we are showing God that we really do mean business. The book of Hebrews, of course, teaches that Jesus is our great high priest, and that we do not need any other intermediary between ourselves and God. But all Christians are members of the priesthood, so we can each

35

use the authority given to us through the Lord to release one another from the burden and consequence of sin (1 Peter 2.5 and Revelation 1.6).

However, if we do on occasions confess to another Christian, we have to be careful and thoughtful about what we say, especially if we are confessing to the very person we have sinned against. A friend came to me very upset because someone had confessed something to her that she wasn't even aware of, and it had hurt her deeply. We need to have a caring attitude to the one we confess to, or we are only removing the weight off our own shoulders and passing it on to someone else!

Besides confessing particular sins to God and telling him we are sorry, we should also look at our motives, our thoughts, and whatever may have tempted us to sin in the first place. We might examine our lifestyle to see if there is anything that consistently leads us into sin. We can then look for ways of avoiding that sort of situation.

Some years ago I noticed that I was often moody and bad-tempered after listening to a radio programme where the characters were constantly arguing. I discovered that their animosity had seeped into my being and affected me! We all know the Lord's Prayer so well, and we pray so often 'lead us not into temptation'. God, of course, does not lead anyone astray: it is our own desires, or wrong thoughts, or misplaced life styles, that put us in a position where we are prey to the temptation to sin.

This leads us on to a third aspect of preparation: forgiveness. Again, we shall find it difficult to experience God's presence while we are brooding on someone else's behaviour to us, or unkind words against us. Forgiveness is not the same as confession, but a step further. We may be very sorry that someone has done something hurtful to us, and we may have confessed any wrong attitude, word or thought on our part. But we still have actively to forgive that person. God desires that, just as he freely forgives men and women their sins, so we too should learn the way of forgiveness: 'Be kind . . . tenderhearted, forgiving one another, as God in Christ forgave you' (Ephesians 4.32).

In a strange way it seems that God expects us to go even further in this matter of forgiving, for whereas he forgives our sins when we confess them to him, he expects us to forgive others even when there is no confession or apparent sense of sorrow on the part of the other person towards us.

If we withold forgiveness from another person, we find that we are the ones who are affected, far more than they. We open ourselves up to many debilitating, unnecessary and harmful emotions such as anger, resentment, fear or hatred. We may find ourselves made angry by what a person has said or done, and be unwilling to let such a strong emotion go down with the evening sun (Ephesians 4.26). We may resent someone who has caused us to lose the prospect of promotion, or who has taken precedence over us in someone else's affections. Stronger emotions like hate and fear can result from unforgivingness, and can fester for many years over things that may have happened to us as a child or young adult. Some emotions are so strong that they seem to have a tangible presence. How many of us have felt tension in a room when we enter it during a quarrel or angry scene? The old expresssion, 'You could cut the air with a knife', is sadly true of many homes in our country today. God wants us to realise that such emotions resulting from unforgiveness cause more hurt to ourselves than to anyone else.

By failing to forgive, we put ourselves in a judgmental position, for we are virtually saying, 'I am right and you are wrong.' Jesus has some very important words to say about this in the Sermon on the Mount, telling us that his way of loving is to turn the other cheek, and not to judge our neighbour. Forgiving others is the way by which we can ensure his forgiveness for ourselves, for 'the measure you give will be the measure you get'. Jesus also said that it is God's prerogative to judge – not ours (John 5.27).

Attitudes of unforgivingness may go back many years,

and may be directed towards things, people or situations, which will really surprise us when we ask the Lord to reveal them. Catherine Marshall discovered some amazing areas of unforgivingness which she describes in her book *Something More*.[1] To her surprise (and ours!) she found she even had a spirit of unforgivingness towards Henry the Eighth, as well as in many other personal matters. Her chapter on forgiveness is based on Mark 11.25; which says, 'Whenever you stand praying, forgive, if you have anything against anyone, so that your Father may forgive you your trespasses.' The Authorised Version says 'aught against any', and these three words cover such a wide range of sins, thoughts actions or words towards an even wider range of people, that we would do well to discover before God where we stand in this matter.

We have already seen that unforgivingness causes more hurt to ourselves than the other person. Scripture teaches us four reasons why we should learn to forgive.

First, when we withhold forgiveness we are no longer righteous, and in fact are placing ourselves in a position where God is far from us. He has not moved – we have done so by our unforgivingness towards another and until we do forgive we should not expect God to answer our prayers: he will not even listen. 'The Lord is far from the wicked, but he hears the prayers of the righteous' (Proverbs 15.29). Confessing our sins, as we saw earlier, and particularly exercising forgiveness if we have 'aught against any', helps to ensure that the Lord hears our prayers and delights in them.

Second, and very important, unless we forgive we will not have our own sins forgiven. We can hardly expect God to do for us something that we are unwilling to do for others. In the Lord's Prayer we are taught to say: 'Forgive us our debts – as we also have forgiven our debtors.' Jesus went on to tell his disciples that if they forgave men their trespasses, their heavenly Father also would forgive them, but if they did not forgive, then neither would God forgive their sins (Matthew 6.14,15). Strong words! But it shows how importantly he views this matter. This alone is reason enough for us to pray, 'Search me O God, and know my heart . . . and see if there be any wicked way in me' (Psalm 139.23–4).

Third, our unforgivingness gives Satan an advantage over us. Paul, in an important little passage in 2 Corinthians 2.5–11, widens the effects of forgiveness to involve other Christians and the effects on the Church. 'Anyone whom you forgive', he wrote to the Christians at Corinth, 'I also forgive. What I have forgiven, if I have forgiven anything, has been for your sake in the presence of Christ, to *keep Satan from gaining the advantage* over us, for we are not ignorant of his designs.'

We may not be the immediate person involved in a hurtful or bad situation – we may be just a friend, a counsellor or an onlooker – but it is just as important for us to forgive as it is for the one directly concerned. This way of living is so important, that if we disregard it we automatically give the devil the advantage over individuals and the Church as a whole. He delights in sowing seeds of anger, hurt and resentment, and in making them grow into large weeds which block our spiritual growth. Forgiveness completely wipes out any hold he has over us in this area, and we can say with Jesus, 'He has no power over me' (John 14.30).

Fourth, unforgivingness on our part can actually lead to ill health: 'Some were sick through their sinful ways, and because of their iniquities suffered affliction' (Psalm 107.17). It is certainly a sin to refuse to forgive someone, and the strong emotions that result can cause sickness to our bodies.

A useful book to read on this subject is *None of These Diseases*,[2] written by a medical doctor who is also a Christian. The book is a fund of information and warnings on the damage we do to our bodies through stress and other factors. Some of the examples he includes are: strong resentment towards another can cause acids to form in our stomachs which in turn may lead to ulcers and other gastric problems; hatred of another produces stress hormones in the body which can result in fatigue; anger can cause contraction of the blood vessels, leading to serious illnesses; arguments can cause raised blood pressure; anxiety and worry can cause stress to the heart; emotional stress can affect the muscles which in turn produce pain – often showing itself in tension headaches. And so the list goes on.

The Lord, our healer, knows very well that if we follow his commandments, especially the commandment to forgive others, we shall be kept free from many of the health problems that plague mankind. We see in the Psalms, too, that forgiveness and healing go hand in hand: 'Bless the Lord . . . who forgives all your iniquity, who heals all your diseases' (Psalm 103.3).

These four reasons to forgive others are for the sake of our own health and well being. It is even more important to forgive people for *their* sake. Our unforgivingness can bind the other person. We see him in a different and wrong way, and probably can't speak naturally to him or act naturally around him. Our heightened senses become aware of each tiny little action either of us makes, because there is a block of unforgivingness binding the relationship.

Peter and I experienced the working out of this principle with our eldest daughter at the end of one school term. She and some friends committed a small misdemeanour. The punishment was rather severe, certainly in proportion to the incident, as it included detention twice on the Monday, and also on the following day – which happened to be Sports Day. I shared with her the importance of confession and forgiveness and how we can bind people with our unforgivingness, and with help she prayed the prayer of forgiveness used at the end of this chapter. I was eager for her homecoming the next day to see what had happened. With a big smile she related how the teacher concerned had changed her mind and only made them do half an hour's detention, so that they were in fact able to see most of the sports. Not only that, but her forgiveness of her teacher so changed her own attitude that she was able to go up to the teacher and wish her goodnight. The teacher responded pleasantly and chatted to her. So we saw the principle working – Tanya forgave, and God worked!

Jesus said, 'I come to bring release to the captives.' How much more do we need to follow his example, and bring release to those we have held in bondage by our unforgivingness.

PRACTICAL

1 Over the course of several days, make a study of your 'aughts and anys'. Divide up your life into segments, e.g. early childhood, first years at school, adolescence, family life, etc., and prayerfully with the Lord go over each area, asking him to show you if there is any unforgivingness towards a person or situation; then actively forgive that person and ask the Lord's healing on them and yourself.

2 Look up James 1.13–15 for God's thoughts on temptation.

PRAYER OF FORGIVENESS[3]

Lord, I release ——— from my judgement. Forgive me that I may have bound him and hampered your work by judging. Now I step out of the way so that heaven can go into action for ———.

NOTES

1 Catherine Marshall, *Something More* (Hodder and Stoughton). Chapter 'Aughts and Anys'.
2 S.I.M. McMillan, *None of These Diseases* (Lakeland).
3 Quoted from *Something More*.

6

The People Involved

You have established the best time and place for your devotions, and have gone into your room. You are now alone with God – just the two of you. But in point of fact there are *four* people in the room – yourself, and the three members of the Trinity: God the Father, God the Son and God the Holy Spirit. They cannot be separated one from the other, for they all belong to each other and with each other. If we make an effort to study their names and their characteristics, then we shall considerably broaden our ability to praise and worship them meaningfully.

One way of experiencing the Persons of the Trinity is by a study of the names which have been used to describe them. There are hundreds of names used in Scripture, and learning even a few will greatly enhance our understanding.

Before we look at the various names of the Trinity, it will be helpful to consider the importance and power of a name. In Old Testament times, the name of a person was an important indication of his personality and character. Even today, expectant parents will hunt through books, choosing a name for their new baby which has a meaning they like. The ancient Pharoahs chose a name for themselves which was very secret and sacred, and known only to themselves. They did not tell another soul this secret title, because it was believed that knowledge of a person's name meant that you had a certain amount of power over them. This is to some extent true – for example, a master in a school class has more authority over his pupils when he can single out an individual by name.

This makes it all the more remarkable that God was willing to give away his name to the people he had created, for by sharing his name he was giving authority to his people. Moses needed the authority of God's name when he was given his great commission to lead the children of Israel out of Egypt. He asked God to reveal his name, and the Lord replied, 'I AM WHO I AM.' God went on to say, 'Say this to the people of Israel, "I AM has sent me to you" . . . This is my name for ever, and thus I am to be remembered throughout all generations' (Exodus 3.14, 15).

It is true that we often tend to become what we are called. If we tell a child he is lazy, he will become like it more and more; tell him he is disobedient and naughty, and he will be discouraged and not make an effort to do better. But tell a child he is loving and helpful, trustworthy and a joy, and he will try to become like that to please us and to hear our praise.

When, as we praise God, we speak out one or more of his many names, all of which have a significant meaning, our thoughts are changed to expect his character to be the same as that implied in the name. The more I call God faithful and true, the more he becomes like that – to me. He already is faithful and true, but the more I reiterate that name, so he becomes faithful and true to me in my expectations of him. In this way my knowledge of God is broadened as I learn more and more of his names.

Names are so important that God sometimes changed them so that a person's new name fitted in with his or her new character; or occasionally the other way round, so that a person's character grew more like their new name. Abram's name originally meant 'a lofty Father', but God changed it to Abraham, meaning 'father of a multitude'. Sarai, his wife, had the meaning 'contentious', yet God changed it to Sarah, meaning 'a princess'. Jacob, the supplanter, became Israel, 'a prince of God'.

In passing, let us remind ourselves that we, too, are given a new name: 'I will give him a white stone, with a new name written on the stone which no one knows, except him who receives it' (Revelation 2.17). Even today, new converts to Christianity in some countries are given a new name, usually at their baptism. This is often because their old names have heathen meanings, and maybe evil connotations, so by taking a new 'Christian' name, they will be encouraged to live a life worthy of that name. Receiving a new name also indicates, of course, a renunciation of the old, past life.

Not only does studying the names of the Trinity increase our vocabulary for praise and worship. We also discover that there is great power in the name of God. Proverbs 18.10 describes the name of the Lord as a strong tower, which will give us protection. This idea is also expressed in the Psalms: 'The name of the God of Jacob protect you' (Psalm 20.1). We can use the name of the Lord to protect us in everyday situations. Catherine Marshall describes one such incident in her book *The Helper*.[1] She tells the true story of a young girl who accepted the offer of a lift from a stranger, thinking he was a neighbour. He drove the car to a remote area outside her town, and it was only when she rebuked him in the name of Jesus that he turned the car round and drove her home without molesting her in any way. How wonderful to know that we all have access to this same power by using the name of the Lord!

As Christians, we must seek to keep the name of God from being dishonoured, both in our lives and in our words. The first of the Ten Commandments is, 'You shall not take the name of your God in vain' (Exodus 20.7). I always used to think that this applied to swearing, and so it probably does; but we must realise also that there is such power and importance attached to the name of God that we should not use it lightly, even in our Christian lives, but reverently and with awe, and with a right understanding of what we are saying. The way we live, our lifestyle, must also reflect the honour due to God's name. If we sin deliberately, even in minor ways like taking stationery from the office, then we are giving a very bad impression of our Lord. 'Let every one who names the name of the Lord depart from iniquity,' said Paul (2 Timothy 2.19).

As well as looking at some of the names and characteristics of each Person of the Trinity, we shall also see how they relate to one another; how we, as God's people, relate to them, and the ways in which they help us.

GOD THE FATHER – WHO HE IS

We probably think of God first as 'our Father', seeing him in his role of bringing all mankind into being. In fact the doctrine of the fatherhood of God is a vital one for many Christians. If you are unfortunate enough to have had a bad experience with your earthly father, then your concept of God as your heavenly father will be tainted.

Rita Bennett, in her book *Emotionally Free*[2], has a chapter entitled 'Parents are Important' in which she says:

> When you were a child, your father was important to you in a way that you may never have thought. He was a prototype of God to you. You drew your picture of what your Father in heaven was like from your father on earth. Since this is so, it is doubly important to have your relationship with him healed. If you haven't, it may have kept you from being open to God at all, or may have saddled you with a false idea of God that distorts your whole approach to him.

In Psalm 68.5, God is described as 'Father of the fatherless' – a wonderful promise for orphans and for those with damaged images of their fathers.

SOME NAMES OF GOD

The fourth word at the beginning of Genesis is 'God' – 'In the beginning, God . . .' This word is *Elohim*, and it is always translated God; it occurs more than 2,500 times in the Bible. *Elohim* is a plural noun, and the meaning and

45

concept behind it is of the plurality of God. So the idea of the Trinity is immediately expressed in the first mention of God in the very first sentence of the Bible. It also means 'fullness of might'.

The name which God gave to Moses – I AM – can also be translated as 'Jehovah', and is the name for the God of Israel. Today it is usually written as Yahweh. It has a wonderful meaning – not just I AM, signifying that God is always here and now, but also 'I will become'. Thus this name holds a tremendous promise of gradual revelation.

The Old Testament gives us a lovely group of names for God the Father. Here are some of them:

Jehovah Jireh means God the Provider (Genesis 22.14)
Jehovah Nissi means God my Banner (Exodus 17.15)
Jehovah Shalom means God my Peace (Judges 6.24)
Jehovah Shammah means God is There (Ezekiel 48.35)
Jehovah Tsidkenu means God our Righteousness (Jeremiah 23.6)

These five names indicate to us that God *is already* our banner, our peace, our provider, and so on; and by the addition of the name Jehovah in front of each, we now have God's assurance that he *will become* these things to us. Five very good reasons to praise him are doubled to ten by God's promise to continue to be these things in the future.

Other biblical names of God include: Holy (Isaiah 57.15); the Lord (Isaiah 42.8); the Father (1 Corinthians 8.6); a Righteous Judge (Psalm 7.11); a Sun and Shield (Psalm 84.11); the Father of spirits (Hebrews 12.9); the Father of lights (James 1.17); Jealous (Exodus 34.14); a Consuming Fire (Hebrews 12.29); and, of course, Love (1 John 4.8,16).

THE WORK OF GOD

God's nature is creative – he loves to design, create and make things. The culmination of this was to create mankind

46

who, he intended, would enjoy him forever. The persons of the Trinity had such love for each other that it naturally spilled over and made them say, 'Let *us* make man in *our* image' (Genesis 1.26). God wanted to enjoy mankind, and to share all his gifts and possessions with us. After the Fall, though man had rejected him, he did not reject mankind. He sought to create a people for himself, and chose the Israelites for 'a people for his own possession' (Deuteronomy 7.6). Through his chosen nation he would show his love to the surrounding tribes and peoples. It is still God's purpose to create a people for himself, and that new people is us – the Church: 'A chosen race, a royal priesthood, a holy nation, God's own people' (1 Peter 2.9).

WHERE IS GOD NOW?

All Scripture tells us that God is in heaven. We have no way of knowing exactly where that is. My dictionary defines it as 'the habitation of God and his angels, usually placed beyond the sky'. Wherever heaven is, the Bible teaches that it is a place separated from mankind. God himself, through his prophet, says, 'Heaven is my throne, and the earth is my footstool' (Isaiah 66.1). The psalmist proclaims: 'The Lord is in his holy temple, the Lord's throne is in heaven' (Psalm 11.4). At the baptism of Jesus, God's voice is heard as 'a voice from heaven, saying "This is my beloved Son" ' (Matthew 3.17). Jesus himself speaks of God as being in heaven, first when he teaches his disciples the Lord's Prayer, and again when he tells his hearers that he will acknowledge those who confess him before his Father who is in heaven (Matthew 6.9 and 10. 32).

WHAT GOD DOES FOR US

It would be very convenient if we could separate the Persons of the Trinity into different compartments, and have clear distinctions as to the exact nature and work of each. However, to our finite minds it is not as clear cut as we would like to think.

47

People in the Old Testament were aware of God only as the One True God – they had no concept of Jesus the Son, or of the promise of the Holy Spirit as he was to be revealed in his fullness at Pentecost. These were only hinted at. So the Old Testament writings give us a clue to the many things that God the Father can be to us. The New Testament tells us even more about God's gifts to his people. These include his love, mercy and comfort, his help, strength, salvation and grace, and eternal life and peace.

Even in this short study of the names and work of God we have discovered a great deal about him, and have found valuable aids to our worship. For instance: we may take the name 'Righteous Judge' and use it in praise to the Lord. It can then form the theme of a prayer, such as: 'Thank you, Father, that you are a righteous judge, that your knowledge and wisdom prevent you from making any mistakes; and that I can freely trust you to make the right decisions and judgements in my life.' In this way your prayer vocabulary is already enhanced as we widen our knowledge of the names of God.

PRACTICAL

Study the following verses for an indication of the many things that God does for us: Exodus 34.6; Leviticus 26.6; 2 Samuel 22.3; Psalm 3.8; Psalm 26.3; Psalm 54.4; Romans 6.23; 2 Corinthians 1.3; James 4.6; 1 John 4.7, 8, 16.

PRAYER

Father, thank you for the many aspects of your character which are revealed to me as I study your many names. May they become a powerful force in my praise and worship and in my prayers.   Amen.

NOTES

1   Catherine Marshall, *The Helper* (Hodder and Stoughton).
2   Rita Bennett, *Emotionally Free* (Kingsway).

7

The Person of Jesus

When we think about Jesus, we think of him first as the Son of God. Probably the best known verse in the Bible is John 3.16: 'God so loved the world that he gave his only Son . . .' The Prologue to John's Gospel says (1.14): 'We have beheld his glory, glory as of the only Son from the Father'; and 1 John 4.9: 'God sent his only Son into the world, so that we might live through him.' Both at the baptism of Jesus and at his transfiguration, the voice of God was heard, saying, 'This is my beloved Son' (Matthew 3.17; Mark 9.7).

Jesus was very conscious of his relationship with the Father: 'I and the Father are one' (John 10.30); 'He who has seen me has seen the Father' (John 14.9). This same thought is later echoed by Paul in Colossians 1.15: 'He is the image of the invisible God.' Paul goes on to tell the Christians at Colossae that in Jesus 'the whole fullness of deity dwells bodily' (2.9).

Jesus, then, is revealed to us in the New Testament as the Son of God, one with the Father in authority and power.

Yet in his incarnation, Jesus divested himself of his divine power. In Paul's words, 'Though he was in the form of God . . . he emptied himself, taking the form of a servant (Philippians 2.6–7). When he came to earth, he came as fully human. Whereas the passages we have already looked at show us his divine nature, elsewhere we find the doctrine of Jesus's complete and full manhood. Yes, he certainly had divine power; but he set this aside in order to become man – the 'man Christ Jesus' who is the 'one mediator between God and man' (1 Timothy 2.5). In his first letter to the Corinthians, Paul takes this thought a stage further by referring to Jesus as the 'second Adam': 'The first Adam became a living being; the last Adam became a life-giving spirit . . . The first man was from the earth, a man of dust; the second man is from heaven' (1 Corinthians 15.45–7). In Romans, he writes that sin came into the world through one man's trespass, but it is through the one man Jesus Christ that we will receive the abundance of grace and the free gift of righteousness (Romans 5.15–17).

Other ways in which the Bible describes the humanity of Jesus are that he 'became flesh and dwelt among us' (John 1.14); and that he shares our nature, our 'flesh and blood' (Hebrews 2.14). We also know that he suffered things common to all mankind: he wept, he was hungry, thirsty, weary and poor.

Jesus had a human body and a human soul: 'My soul is very sorrowful, even unto death (Matthew 26.38); 'Now is my soul troubled' (John 12.27). The prophecy foretelling the death of Jesus in Isaiah 53 speaks of him 'pouring out his soul to death'.

The fact of the humanity of Jesus is comforting for us. If his perfect and sinless life on earth was lived through his divine power, it would have no relevance for us and we would be completely unable to emulate it. He could have sailed through the horror and agony of the cross in a supernatural body that felt no pain, terror or heartache. But because he was made like us in every way, and 'because he himself has suffered and been tempted, he is able to help those who are tempted' (Hebrews 2.18). There is nothing that you and I can experience that Jesus has not already experienced in one form or other.

But the amazing truth and wonder of Jesus's life lived as an ordinary man is the fact that he did have power – power that came upon him at his baptism in the form of the Holy Spirit – and that same power is available to every Christian.

Jesus came to earth to show us that mankind can live perfectly in tune with God. After his time of testing in the wilderness, he returned 'in the power of the Spirit' to live his perfect life. It was through that same power that he was able to perform his healings and miracles. This truth becomes even more wonderful when we realise that through the same indwelling Holy Spirit we, too, are able to resist temptation and live the kind of life that Jesus did.

SOME NAMES OF JESUS

The concordance in the back of my Bible has at least 110 names for Jesus – the second person of the Trinity. Obviously there are far too many to deal with here, but we can at least look at some of them and the significance of their meanings.

The actual name 'Jesus' means 'Jehovah is salvation'. When the angel told Joseph that Mary would bear a son, he said, 'You shall call his name Jesus, for he will save his people from their sins' (Matthew 1.21). Understanding the meaning behind the name of Jesus brings to life Peter's words in Acts 4.12: 'There is no other name under heaven given among men by which we must be saved.' The many religions of the world seek to show different ways of reaching God, but it is only in the name of Jesus that we shall find salvation.

Jesus also has another name – Christ, 'the Anointed One'. (This is Greek for Messiah, which means the same thing.) It was Peter who, after three years of living and working with Jesus, finally realised who Jesus was: 'You are the Christ, the Son of the living God' (Matthew 16.16).

Three more names that often run together in our minds are Prophet, Priest and King. Christ was predicted as a prophet way back in Deuteronomy 18.15: 'The Lord your God will raise up for you a prophet like me from among you, from your brethren – him you shall heed.' After his resurrection, Jesus appeared to two disciples walking along the Emmaus road. Their eyes were kept from recognising

51

him, and they started explaining to him the things concerning Jesus of Nazareth' who was a prophet mighty in deed and word before God and all the people' (Luke 24.13–27).

A prophet is someone who speaks forth a message which has been communicated to him through divine inspiration; and Jesus, more than anyone, was able to tell his hearers the words and messages of God (John 12.49). Jesus refers to himself as a prophet after teaching in his own home synagogue and getting little response: 'A prophet is not without honour except in his own country and in his own house' (Matthew 13.57).

The second in this trilogy of names is Priest; and the book of Hebrews has much to say on the priestly work that Jesus has carried out for us. Because complete perfection was never attainable through the old order of Levitical priests, God made away with it and replaced it with a new way of grace. Not only that: the former priests, being mortal, could not exercise a permanent priesthood. But Jesus holds his priesthood for ever, because he continues for ever (Hebrews 7.24). Likewise, Jesus has no need to offer a daily sacrifice, for he did this once and for all on the cross (Hebrews 7.27). Mark's Gospel (15.38) records how, immediately after Jesus breathed his last, 'the curtain of the temple was torn in two from top to bottom.' The curtain hung in front of the Holy of Holies where the High Priest only went once a year to make atonement for the people (Leviticus chapter 16). The fact that Jesus has now made the one perfect and complete sacrifice for our sins means that we have free access into the Holy of Holies, the presence of God; we do not have to wait, we can go in at any time, because Jesus, our great High Priest, has gone before us and broken the dividing wall (or curtain) that separated us from God (Ephesians 2.14).

The New Testament contains many references to Jesus as King; and of course he preached many times that the kingdom of God has come upon us (Matthew 12.28) and is in the midst of us (Luke 17.21). At the time of Christ, the

Jewish nation was under the control of the Roman Empire. The Jews, quite naturally, were looking for someone to rescue them and set them free. They were, in fact, looking for a king. When Jesus came, preaching about the kingdom of God, many people, including the Scribes and Pharisees and other religious leaders, thought that he was the king who would rescue them physically and materially. But this was not part of God's plan. In John 6.15 we read how Jesus had to withdraw to the mountain by himself, for he 'perceived that they were about to come and take him by force to make him king'. As he told Pilate at his trial, his kingdom was 'not of this world' (John 18.36).

As we begin to understand the significance of Jesus as Prophet, Priest and King, we find we have three more ways of praising him, and applying these truths to our own lives.

Other biblical names of Jesus include: the Way, the Truth and the Life (John 14.6); the Good Shepherd (John 10.11); the Vine (John 15.1,5); the Light of the World (John 8.12). He is also described as the Son of man (Matthew 13.41, Acts 7.56 and Matthew 8.20); as our brother (Mark 3.35); and our friend (John 15.15).

All these names give scope for meditation as we widen our knowledge and understanding of the character of our Lord Jesus Christ.

THE WORK OF JESUS

The chief work of Jesus for humankind was to die for the sins of the world, and in so doing to reconcile men and women to the Father. Our relationship with God was broken at the Fall, and it needed the second Adam, Christ, to restore the relationship. Even while the Scribes and Pharisees were planning how to get rid of Jesus, it was Caiaphas, the High Priest, who 'prophesied that Jesus should die for the nation, and not for the nation only, but to gather into one the children of God who are scattered abroad' (John 11.51).

WHERE IS JESUS NOW?

Jesus repeatedly told his disciples that he was going away – back to the Father. He had to say it many times, but even then they didn't understand. But it was necessary for our sakes that Jesus should go back to heaven in order that he could send the Holy Spirit upon his disciples and followers.

Many of the Bible writers tell us that Jesus is now in heaven, with the Father. 'Jesus, after he had spoken to them, was taken up into heaven and sat down at the right hand of God' (Mark 16.19). 'Seek the things that are above, where Christ is, seated at the right hand of God,' says Paul (Colossians 3.1). Other references are given at the end of this chapter for you to study. A really wonderful thought arises from the frequent use of the word 'sat' or 'seated' to describe Jesus' position. Not only is Jesus in heaven, but he is *seated*. When do you sit down? Usually when you have finished your work – you can sit and rest and relax. This was exactly so for Jesus. His last words on the cross were, 'It is finished' (John 19.30). The work he had to do and the role he came to fulfill were completed. He could return to the Father and sit down to rest after his labours, though he continues to care for us till the time is ready for his return, and until all his enemies are put under his feet (Mark 12.35–7).

But this truth is only part of the glorious whole. It becomes even more wonderful to us when we read that God has 'raised us up with him, and *made us sit with him* in the heavenly places in Christ Jesus' (Ephesians 2.6). Yes, we are still living a life down here on earth, but the other side of the coin is that 'your life is hid with Christ in God' (Colossians 3.3); so it follows that where Christ is – so am I.

When we see ourselves seated with Christ in heaven, we have a transformed attitude to life, and a totally different viewpoint. Instead of floundering down here, in the middle of life's difficulties and problems, we can, by faith, visualise ourselves seated next to Jesus and the Father, and have a new perspective and awareness of our problems. For a start, they won't seem so big, and we shall be able to see them in their true light. And because we are seated at the powerhouse of God, we can direct that power through our prayers on to the situations that need it. This is why we are told to set our minds on things above.

WHAT JESUS DOES FOR US IN HEAVEN

'Jesus . . . always lives to make intercession' (Hebrews 7.25); 'Christ Jesus . . . who is at the right hand of God, who indeed intercedes for us' (Romans 8.34). When Jesus was on earth he spent much of his time praying – especially for his followers. He still continues this work of intercession in heaven. He is acting as our advocate, or go-between, before his Father, explaining to him our circumstances and lives, bringing to him our problems and worries, and the ways in which we need help and healing. Not that the Father (our Father) is unaware of our condition, or unwilling to give us what we need, but rather that the Father and Son are united in their interest and care for us. To know that Jesus is interceding for us is especially comforting at those times when we feel that no one else knows about our problems or difficult circumstances. We can picture Jesus interceding for us with God the Father, putting our 'case' before him far more eloquently than we can. 'I am praying for them', Jesus said (John 17.9), and he still continues to do so now.

Another thing that Jesus does for us in heaven is to 'present' us 'without blemish before the presence of his glory' (Jude 24). Similar references are found in Ephesians 5.27 and Colossians 1.22. We can only get the full impact of this glorious fact when we begin to visualise its full meaning in our minds. I like to imagine Jesus leading me into the Father's presence, one arm around my shoulders and saying to his Father: 'May I now present Jean to you, she is holy, blameless and without any blemish, and is suitable therefore to remain in our company.'

55

There are so many other things that Jesus is doing for us, too. For instance: he gives us eternal life (John 3.15); he forgives (Acts 5.31); he heals (Acts 3.16); he judges (Acts 10.42). The theme is a rich field for study in our quiet times.

We have so much to thank God for in sending us his Son, Jesus Christ, to die for us on the cross. How wonderful, too, to have so many truths revealed to us when we study the many names of Jesus.

PRACTICAL

1 Further verses to study under 'Where is Jesus now?': Acts 2.32–35, Hebrews 9.24 and 1 Timothy 6.16.
2 With the help of your concordance make a further study of names of Jesus that we have not covered here.

PRAYER

Thank you, Father, for sending your son Jesus to die for me on the cross. Thank you that even now he is interceding on my behalf in your presence, and that one day he will return with all glory and majesty, might and power. Amen.

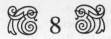

8

The Person of the Holy Spirit

Now we are going to look at the third Person of the Trinity – and I say 'person' deliberately. Many people still have the impression that the Holy Spirit is an 'it', and devoid of personality. It grieved me recently to hear someone referring to him as 'it' when praying in church. By degrading him in this way we are denying his glory; and we are denying ourselves the joy of his presence and robbing ourselves of the power he gives us to live the Christ-like life.

Catherine Marshall says of the Holy Spirit: 'The Helper is a Person – one of the three persons of the Godhead. As such, he possesses all the attributes of personality. He has a mind (Romans 8.27), he has knowledge (1 Corinthians 2.10, 11) and he has a will (1 Corinthians 12.11).'[1]

The third person of the Trinity is the Spirit of God himself, for through Ezekiel (36.26–27) God promised that not only will he give us a new heart, but he will also put his Spirit within us. In Isaiah we read that God the Father will send his Spirit upon the promised Messiah (chapter 61.1–2); and the response of Jesus was to quote this very passage the first time he preached in the synagogue at Nazareth where he had been brought up: 'The Spirit of the Lord is upon me, because he has anointed me to preach good news to the poor . . . to proclaim release to the captives . . .' (Luke 4.18).

God, the Father, not only poured out his Spirit on Jesus, but it is his purpose to give him to all mankind: 'And it shall come to pass afterward, that I will pour out my spirit on all flesh' (Joel 2.28). So, when a person tells God that he is willing to receive his Son as Saviour, the Father also promises the Spirit. The Joel prophecy first became fact for the Church when, as recorded in the book of Acts, the disciples, in obedience to the command of Jesus, were waiting in Jerusalem until 'you shall receive power when the Holy Spirit has come upon you'. On that amazing day of Pentecost, when everyone in the city was bewildered at the many languages coming out of the mouths of unlearned fishermen, it was Peter who stood up and told the crowds that this was simply the fulfilment of prophecy.

SOME NAMES OF THE SPIRIT

As with the Father and the Son, the Spirit is given a great many names and descriptions in Scripture. Here are just a few: Comforter (John 14.26 – in some translations); Counsellor (John 14.15; 16.7); Guide (John 16.13); Holiness (Romans 1.4); Creator, Renewer (Psalm 104.30); Judgement (Isaiah 4.4); Wisdom, Understanding, Counsel, Might, Knowledge (Isaiah 11.2); Truth (John 16.13). He is described as a dove (Matthew 3.16); fire (Acts 2.3); wind (John 3.8); living water (John 7.38–9), and in many other ways. When we study and ponder on these names, we will be amply rewarded by a new awareness of the personality and power of the Holy Spirit.

THE WORK OF THE SPIRIT

When Jesus told his disciples about the coming Counsellor, he explained to them that one of his roles would be 'to glorify me' and 'to bear witness to me'. The Holy Spirit therefore has the function of exalting Jesus and lifting him up before the eyes of the world so that people will be drawn to him, and so find salvation.

Another work of the Spirit is to convince people of their sin (John 16.8-11). This is why, however hard we try, we can never convert another soul to the Lord – that ability belongs to the Spirit alone. But we can work in harmony with the Spirit, by directing his power through prayer to those who need salvation.

WHERE THE SPIRIT IS NOW

It is clear from what Jesus said, according to John's Gospel chapters 14–16, that the Spirit is within us. He is no longer confined to heaven, for he has been sent to live in every believer – and not just for a short while but for ever (14.16).

All who believe and trust in Jesus as Saviour have received the Holy Spirit. The moment we become Christians the Holy Spirit comes to live within us – otherwise we would not be able to acknowledge Jesus as our Lord. Paul explained to the Corinthians that 'No one can say "Jesus is Lord" except by the Holy Spirit' (1 Corinthians 12.3). Peter preached on the Day of Pentecost that repentance and baptism go hand in hand with receiving the Holy Spirit: 'Repent, and be baptised every one of you in the name of Jesus Christ for the forgiveness of your sins; and you shall receive the gift of the Holy Spirit (Acts 2.38).

Some people receive such a deep infilling of the Spirit at their conversion that their lives are dramatically changed. They may find that he has given them the power instantly to abandon sinful behaviour, to stop bad habits such as swearing or smoking, and to gain victory over 'the lusts of the flesh'. Accompanying this may well be some of the gifts of the Spirit mentioned in 1 Corinthians 12 and Ephesians 4. For others, the Spirit's influence in their lives is very gentle and, though changes occur, they may not be aware that it is the Holy Spirit within them prompting them and empowering them. It is a sad fact, though, that many new believers know little or nothing about the work of the Holy Spirit in their lives, and do not get beyond the stage of repentance and baptism. Paul saw an example of this when he went to Ephesus. He found some disciples there and asked them if they had received the Holy Spirit when they believed. Their reply was that they had never even heard that there was a Holy Spirit (Acts 19.2).

As we grow as Christians we shall find ourselves learning more about the ministry of the Holy Spirit in our lives, through teaching, through studying Scripture, or through the testimony of others. If we were not taught about the Holy Spirit at the time of our conversion, we may well come to see our need to have 'less of self and more of him' as the hymn writer puts it; or we may experience a desire for some of the gifts of the Spirit, such as tongues, healing, prophecy, interpretation, and so on. Some people then have an experience sometimes referred to as 'the baptism of the Spirit' or 'being filled with the Spirit', which is a time when we specifically ask the Holy Spirit to come into our lives in a new way. This is also sometimes spoken of as a 'second blessing' – though we are not limited as to the number of times we can ask the Holy Spirit to fill us anew. Indeed, Scripture implies that it is a continuing, on-going process; as our awareness and desire for the Holy Spirit grows, so we can go on asking to be filled with more and more of his power.

I like to think of my body and personality as a house, with many different rooms, one or two of which were already filled with the Spirit at my conversion. The Lord Jesus is King there, but there are many other rooms, or parts of my life, where I am still in control and where the Spirit does not yet have full sway.

When I became aware that the Holy Spirit was not in every area of my life, I was encouraged by others to ask for and seek more of him, and to enter into the joy of receiving his spiritual and supernatural gifts. I had to be willing for the Lord to take full control of my life, then come to Jesus and ask him for this most precious of all the Father's gifts. For Jesus promised: 'If you who are evil know how to give good gifts to your children, how much more will the heavenly Father give the Holy Spirit to those who ask him!' (Luke 11.13).

So, one Saturday evening some years ago, I asked the Lord for a deeper filling of the Holy Spirit. Nothing happened outwardly. I did not speak in tongues, or notice any other change. I had, however, been counselled that, when I asked for the Holy Spirit to come in his fullness, it should be in a similar way to when I received salvation – 'by faith' (Galatians 3.5). So I thanked the Lord on that Saturday evening that he had already filled me with his Holy Spirit, accepted the fact by faith, and believed that I would see the evidence of his gifts in the coming days. And so it was, for the following week, after sharing my experience with a group of people with whom I was praying, my vicar laid hands on me and my mouth was then released to praise God in a new language. Since then I have found that the Spirit has released other parts of my life, especially with regard to praise and worship, and understanding the Scriptures.

My experience of receiving the fullness of the Spirit came many years after my conversion. This was partly due to the fact that I had received little or no teaching about the Holy Spirit in my earlier years. When people are taught the complete gospel at the time of their conversion (as in Peter's sermon in Acts 2), they are able to receive the Holy Spirit immediately, in all his fullness and power, and can be spared the years of waiting that many have experienced.

When we have the Spirit within us, we have the personality and characteristics and the presence of Jesus. That is why we can say 'we have the mind of Christ' (1 Corinthians 2.16), and why Paul could say, 'It is no longer I who live, but Christ who lives in me' (Galatians 2.20). Jesus's body is in heaven, but his power and personality live within us through the indwelling Holy Spirit.

WHAT THE HOLY SPIRIT DOES FOR US

The Holy Spirit has several ministries to bring to the Christian.

First, he gives us power. Even Jesus did not begin his earthly ministry until he had received the baptism of the Holy Spirit at the river Jordan. He then went straight into the wilderness for forty days and was tempted by the devil. Following that encounter he returned 'in the power of the Spirit' to begin his work of teaching and healing, followed by signs and miracles. He told his disciples that they, too, would have power to heal and witness, teach and cast out demons, through the same indwelling Holy Spirit. In fact, he said, they would do even greater works than he, because he was returning to the Father, and would send the Holy Spirit to them (John 14.12).

So many of us try to live the Christian life in our own strength, not realising that the power of God is available to us through the Holy Spirit. When our eldest daughter was thirteen she confided to me that she had 'stopped being a Christian' because she was finding it too hard at school being the odd one out. She was very upset, and it had weighed on her heart for many months. Sharing her trouble with me brought her great relief, so that she felt able to attend the school Christian Union the next day, and has continued following the Lord ever since. But this experience made me realise that she had been trying to witness for the Lord in her own strength, and had not been aware that the Holy Spirit could give her his power.

Another ministry of the Holy Spirit is to teach us 'all things' (John 14.26) – in fact 'teacher' is one of his names. This is especially relevant in our Bible study. Because the Bible was written through the guidance and inspiration of God (2 Timothy 3.16), it is only logical to expect that the one who will teach us and help us to understand it is the Spirit of God. The Holy Spirit can speak directly to our spirits and reveal God's word to us, teaching us new truths.

He also teaches us things we have not known before – he is the prophetic word of God, telling us of things in the future (John 16.13). Old Simeon in the temple had had it revealed to him by the Spirit that he would not die until he had seen the Christ (Luke 2.26).

The Holy Spirit will also give us words to speak, especially in difficult circumstances, when we are faced with enemies, or when we are being questioned about our faith: 'Do not be anxious how or what you are to answer or what you are to say,' Jesus told his disciples, 'for the Holy Spirit will teach you in that very hour what you ought to say' (Luke 12.11–12).

Besides instructing us from the Word of God, the Holy Spirit also helps us to remember the words of Jesus (once we have read them, of course!). Jesus himself promised this: 'He will teach you all things, and bring to your remembrance all that I have said to you.' But Christians have discovered that this 'remembering' extends far wider than the spiritual realm, and into our everyday lives and circumstances. I am still in the process of learning that if I, or the children, lose something, then it is no good getting angry and wasting time hunting all over the house. It is far better to hand the situation over to the Spirit and allow him to reveal the 'hiding place' in his own time and way. He never fails!

The Spirit also intercedes for us, and helps us to pray. How wonderful to realise that we have two advocates – Jesus in heaven interceding for us, and the Holy Spirit interceding within. Two immeasurably powerful helpers! 'The Spirit helps us in our weakness: for we do not know how to pray as we ought, but the Spirit himself intercedes for us with sighs too deep for words' (Romans 8.26).

The list of all that the Holy Spirit does for us seems to go on for ever! Because he is the Spirit of God, he brings our spirits into the presence of God, and enables us to worship him 'in spirit and in truth'. He also brings us into a whole new experience of the supernatural realm, with gifts such as speaking in tongues (Acts 2.4,11); prophecies (Acts 19.6); visions and dreams (Acts 2.17); as well as love (Romans 5.5). He enables us to praise God, and inspires us with joy (1 Thessalonians 1.6).

WHY WE NEED THE TRINITY

Everything I need to be a fulfilled Christian is embodied in the three Persons of the Trinity. I need all three Persons to be a complete person myself. I am lacking if I know only God the Father, as some religions do, for I cannot come to him unless it is through the Son – Jesus (John 14.6). I may know only the Father and the Son, but I am lacking in power if I am not aware that this gift of power is available through the Holy Spirit within me. My ability to draw upon the power of God and the resources of heaven is weakened if I do not know the Spirit in person, and if I have not given over every area of my life to him. I need all three members of the Trinity to help me with their many gifts and ministries.

Now that we are more aware of the names, characters and ministries of the Persons of the Trinity, we shall be far better able to praise them as they so richly deserve.

PRACTICAL

If you have not done so already, begin to seek for the full power of the Holy Spirit in your life. Study and read as much as you can about him, then seek out someone to pray with you.

PRAYER

Father, thank you so much that because Jesus died on the cross for me, rose victorious and now reigns with you, I can now come into your presence through the Holy Spirit who lives in me. I rejoice in the power of the many names of the Trinity. Thank you that knowing them helps me in my Christian life, and enables me to praise you more.   Amen.

NOTE

1   Catherine Marshall, *The Helper* (Hodder and Stoughton).

9

Making a Joyful Noise

Now we will begin to look in closer detail at some elements that can be incorporated into our quiet time with the Lord. I find that an essential part of my meeting with him is the part I spend in vocal praise and worship. For many years my quiet times consisted solely of Bible study and prayer. I had no idea that the Lord also wanted me to use this opportunity regularly to praise and worship him. Immediately I began to do so, however, my quiet times became alive, with an increased sense of his presence.

Soon he was showing me from his word many new and exciting ways to worship and praise, pray and study. I discovered that one of the keys to entering straight into his presence was by deliberately using my mouth, lips and tongue, actually speaking out loud words of praise and adoration. Praising God leads us into the holy of holies in a tangible way, and makes us more aware of God's majesty. It also builds up and increases our confidence, so that when we come to prayer and intercession later on we can be sure that he hears us. We have seen that we have a marvellous opportunity of giving something to God, instead of always being on the receiving end. The very reason we exist is to 'live for the praise of his glory' (Ephesians 1.12); we therefore need to see that praising God with our lips and mouths is important to him, and a blessing to us.

I have prefaced most of the following elements with the dictionary definition, as I personally found this was helpful in separating and identifying them, and enabled me to use each element more effectively.

PRAISE

Praise, verb. Express warm approbation of, commend the merits of (person, thing); glorify, extol the attributes of (God, etc.).

Psalm 145.3: Great is the Lord, and greatly to be praised.

Most of us find it difficult to praise God, at least to begin with. This is very often simply because we don't know what to say! During a time of praise in a housegroup meeting I noticed that our prayers of praise soon turned into prayers of thanksgiving, simply because we ran out of appropriate words and phrases. Obviously there is a fine line to be drawn between praise and thanks; but basically we praise God for who he *is*, and we thank him for the things he *does* – or has done or is going to do. This is where our study of the names and character of God is helpful, for it gives us a fund of knowledge out of which to praise him.[1] Praising God as 'creator', for example, in all the many aspects of this wonderful attribute, could keep us going for two or three minutes at least. So we need not just be limited to such phrases as 'Praise the Lord' or 'Hallelujah'!

I have also found it helpful to discover how people in the Bible praised God: Hannah, David, Mary and Zechariah are all good examples in their different circumstances.[2] Studying the ways in which they praised God gives us further ideas of how to go about this important aspect of devotion.

We cannot enter glibly into praising God, for it takes time and effort on our part to praise him as he deserves and requires. In fact Hebrews 13.15 even speaks of a 'sacrifice of praise', which gives us an insight into its true nature.

On occasion I like to take a Psalm of praise and read it out loud to the Lord. At other times I meditate on one or two aspects of his personality and character, and praise him for such attributes.

Recently a group of five or six of us got together to practise and experiment with this element. One way we have tried is for all of us to speak out words of praise aloud together. Obviously, we felt self-conscious about doing this at first, but the more we practised it the more natural it became. One evening Peter had to leave us to collect our eldest daughter from an evening out, and the rest of us promised to praise the Lord together and not stop till he came back. We started by singing a hymn, then each of us in turn began praising God aloud in different words and phrases. I found I was really stretched into thinking about what I was saying, and was greatly encouraged to realise that the more I spoke out, the more new words and phrases of praise came into my mind. We discovered, that evening, that praise generates more praise. When we finally stopped, on Peter's return, we were all exhilarated and thrilled at this new step forward that we had taken together.

However, before any of us can get into such a situation of praising with other people, we need to have made it a natural part of our personal daily times with the Lord, and certainly it is one of the most important elements to practise and include in our quiet times.

WORSHIP

Worship, verb. Adore as divine, pay religious homage to; regard with adoration. Noun. Worthiness, merit, honour and respect; reverent homage or service paid to God.

Exodus 34.14: 'Thou shalt worship no other god.'

God has planted in all mankind the seed of worship. He has certainly created a space in our hearts for him alone to fill; but so often the Lord's place is filled by other gods and idols such as money, work, home, garden, cars and so on. We read in Exodus 34.14 that God is a jealous God and will have no other gods given priority over him. The reason he calls us to worship him is, of course, that he is the one true God. The Psalmist says: 'O come let us worship and bow down and kneel before the Lord our maker', and that shows us the state of awe and adoration that our hearts should be in as we honour and respect him.

BLESSING

Bless, verb. Consecrate; call holy, adore (God); invoke God's favour on; pronounce words that bring supernatural favour upon (of father, priest, etc.).

Psalm 103.1: Bless the Lord, O my soul; and all that is within me, bless his holy name!

We may find it strange to think in terms of us mortals being able to bless God, as we usually associate blessing as coming from God to us. However, the Lord in his gracious love has made us kings and priests and joint heirs with Christ, and it would seem that we do have this ability to bless God, as Scripture indicates. Not only that; the Psalmist tells us to bless the Lord at all times and for his praise to be continually in our mouth (Psalm 34.1). The more we praise the Lord, the more we shall find ourselves blessing his holy name.

THANKSGIVING

Thank, verb. Express gratitude to (person for thing).
Thanksgiving, noun. Expression of gratitude, esp. to God.

1 Chronicles 16.34: O give thanks to the Lord, for he is good.

We all have ample reasons to give thanks to God for the many things he has done for us or given to us. We could probably go on for hours thanking him for his many blessings and gifts to us personally. As we look back on each day and thank him for daily loading us with benefits, we will find our minds enlarged and widened as we see his involvement in so many areas of our lives. Thus thanksgiving gains momentum the more we practise it.

It delights God's heart even more, though, when we begin to thank him, not just for what he has already done, but for what we believe he is going to do. Thanking God in advance is a valuable way of increasing our faith as we pray and intercede for ourselves and the world.

SINGING

Sing, verb. Utter words, in tuneful succession; produce vocal melody.

Ephesians 5.19: Addressing one another in psalms and hymns and spiritual songs, singing and making melody to the Lord with all your heart.

Singing is probably one of the easiest and most natural ways for us to praise the Lord. When I began to take my quiet times seriously, I found it was also the most effective way to enter the Lord's presence and to sense him near me. Singing to the Lord was the avenue by which I entered the throne room. After singing for five or ten minutes, I found that I became aware of the presence of God in a quiet but tangible way, and I tried not to go on to prayer or study till I had reached this stage.

There are many different ways of singing to the Lord. First, there are hymns. We have many old and beautifully written hymns to choose from, and their value should not be lost in the joy of the lovely new songs and choruses that we are learning. Old and new each have a valuable part to play in our singing repertoires. Then we can be adventurous, and vary our singing by taking a Psalm of praise and singing it – perhaps to a tune we already know, or one that comes to us as we sing; this may be something like a Gregorian chant, which was one of the earliest forms of church music. Of course, this is where a hymn book or chorus book will come in handy, and why it is useful to keep them with our Bibles and the other tools mentioned in a previous chapter.

There are several important reasons why we should sing to God regularly – even on our own in our quiet times. Singing can be a great help when we are not really in the mood to sit down with the Lord. Singing to him releases our spirits and by-passes the way we feel. Contact with the Holy

Spirit through singing God's praises releases our own spirits and affects our whole being and personality, so that we find that we are being led by the Spirit, and not by the flesh, and our feelings and emotions are affected from the inside through our spirits, rather than from the outside through our souls and bodies.

Singing also generates faith. When we sing to God about his goodness, love and faithfulness, our level of expectancy automatically rises.

Singing has always been an important aspect of worshipping God. At the installation of the Temple in Jerusalem, certain people were appointed especially for the job of singing. Their work was considered important enough to set them free from any other duties. It was also a demanding task, for they were on duty day and night (1 Chronicles 9.33).

The Lord once made use of the singing voice in a remarkable way which is described in 2 Chronicles 20.21: he used it as a powerful weapon. In fact, it was King Jehoshaphat's secret weapon, for instead of bringing out his crack troops, or horses and riders, or his foot soldiers, it was the singers who were put in the front line, and 'as they began to sing and praise', so the Lord set an ambush against the enemy and the Moabites and Ammonites were routed. A remarkable picture of the seeming foolishness of God confounding the enemy! We are told in Ephesians that 'we are not contending against flesh and blood, but against the principalities, against the powers, against the world rulers of this present darkness, against the spiritual hosts of wickedness in the heavenly places' (Ephesians 6.12). When we sing to God and praise him, we are proclaiming to the devil and all his hosts that God is King of kings and Lord of all.

MUSIC AND MELODY

Music, noun. Art of combining sounds with a view to beauty of form and expression of emotion.

70

Melody, noun. Sweet music; musical arrangement of words; arrangement of single notes in musically expressive succession.

2 Chronicles 7.6: The priests stood at their posts; the Levites also, with the instruments for music to the Lord which King David had made for giving thanks to the Lord.

Those who can play a musical instrument clearly have an added gift to use in praising the Lord. Unfortunately, the most I can do is tap a tambourine! Even that, though, can add to the praise we give to the Lord in our quiet time.

Musicians who have their instruments with them as they praise the Lord may even find that he will give them new songs or tunes. It is very often in such an attitude of worship and praise that creativity and inspiration come.

Just as the singers in the Old Testament had a special role to play in the services of the Temple, so too did the musicians, and this is dramatically portrayed in 2 Chronicles 5.11–14: because of the joint praise of the musicians, singers and priests 'the glory of the Lord filled the house of God' and the priests could not stand to minister because of the cloud of the Lord's presence!

WORSHIP TAPES AND RECORDS

Even though we may not have the gift of making our own music, listening to recorded worship songs is a sure way of lifting us into the Lord's presence. We can use these as part of our time of praise, joining in with the tape or record, in unison or even harmonising. (By doing this I have also begun to grow more confident in harmonising in church or a meeting). Listening to such music can have a very powerful effect, as one member of our housegroup can testify. After several months of depression, and much prayer on her behalf, someone suggested she should listen to worship tapes. Since she found that the worst time of all was the early morning her husband started playing a worship tape first thing, so that when she woke up it was to hear the Lord being praised. Gradually, over the next few days her

71

condition began to improve, and the more she listened, the more she was able to cope with her morning lethargy. Now, though she is fully healed, whenever I visit her, or even telephone, I can hear Christian music on in the background, and it has become an important part of her life.

Scripture has a similar story to tell regarding King Saul. We read in 1 Samuel 16.23 that God removed his Spirit from Saul, and sometimes an evil spirit came upon him, making him moody and irritable. Then it was that David took the lyre and played it with his hand, so Saul was refreshed and was well, and the evil spirit departed from him.

SPEAKING IN TONGUES

Gift of tongues. Power of speaking in unknown tongues, esp. as miraculously conferred on early Christians.

Acts 2.4: They were all filled with the Holy Spirit and began to speak in other tongues, as the Spirit gave them utterance.

If you are a new Christian, you may have very little knowledge of what speaking in tongues is all about. Basically, it is a way of speaking to God in a language we have never learned. This gift of tongues is often received when people enter into the experience of receiving the baptism of the Spirit, though one can enter into the fullness of the Spirit without receiving tongues at all, or perhaps not until months or years later.[3] Tongues may either be a language of earth, as was the experience of the disciples at Pentecost (Acts 2.7–11), or it can be a heavenly language which has no known counterpart on earth.

The great New Testament chapter on the use of tongues is 1 Corinthians 14. Here Paul speaks about two different ways in which tongues can be used. One is in public, when there should ideally (and as directed by Scripture) be an interpretation (verse 13), and the other is used in our private devotions. Paul confesses in verse 18 that he speaks in tongues more than any of his readers. He clearly used this gift a great deal in his own personal devotions, and probably at other times of the day as well, and found it so beneficial that he wanted all his readers to share in its blessings.

As speaking in tongues has been a fairly controversial subject of recent years, many Christians may be hesitant to explore this area. Let us remember again that God is Spirit, and once we have entered into a spiritual relationship with him it is only 'natural' that we should begin to experience 'supernatural' happenings in our lives.

One of the reasons we may have difficulties with this subject is that we tend to want to hang on to parts of our lives. Even when we believe that we are willing to let God be Lord over every area, we may still find that we want to hold on to one last thing – and that is the control of our tongue. James points out that no human being can tame the tongue, but by letting God have full use of this organ we are also showing him that he may have full control of our lives (James 3.6–10).

There are three main reasons why Christians have found the gift of tongues so helpful, and when we understand these we shall see that the gift is one to be desired and not spurned out of fear or misunderstanding.

First, we can use our tongue to praise God. We have already seen how important praise is, and what it can do to widen our vocabulary and understanding. But there may still come a point when we run out of words, and here is where our spiritual language can play its part; we can use tongues to continue praising the Lord in a way that is pure and direct. It is interesting to note that when the apostles received the Spirit on the day of Pentecost, the comment from the people around was, 'we hear them telling in our own tongues the *mighty works of God*' (Acts 2.11).

Secondly, speaking in tongues builds up the individual believer. Scripture is very clear about this important aspect of using our spiritual language. Paul tells us (in 1 Corinthians 14.4) that 'he who speaks in a tongue edifies (builds up) himself.' It is something we shall probably not be consciously aware of, certainly to begin with; but again we are dealing with the spiritual realm, so we can hardly be surprised that it is such a blessing to the individual Christian.

Thirdly, tongues can be used in our times of prayer and intercession. It is especially helpful if we feel that the Lord is asking us to pray for someone, but we don't know the circumstances, or that person's present situation. Praying in tongues opens the channel for God to work, and because we know it is God's own Spirit praying through us, then we can be confident that we are praying in the will of God, and therefore that the prayer will be answered.

An important point to note is that, when we pray in tongues, we are speaking directly to God himself, who created our tongues and voices in the first place. 'For one who speaks in a tongue speaks not to men – but to God' (1 Corinthians 14.2).

To make it easier to make progress in this area, it helps if we pray aloud during our times of prayer and intercession, so that we get used to the sound of our own voice. We can hardly expect God to give us the gift of tongues if we are not making our tongues, mouths and vocal cords available to speak out loud in the first place! The Lord doesn't suddenly take over our voices, but he uses them as we begin to speak out.

Jacky Pullinger, in her book *Chasing the Dragon*, tells how she used her gift of tongues each day as she walked round Hong Kong among the drug addicts.[4] She was advised to practise her gift each day for fifteen minutes till it became a natural part of her daily life, and she describes in her book the practical benefits of using tongues. This may also be the secret of 'praying at all times in the Spirit' (Ephesians 6.18), for it is possible to be praying in tongues in our minds while we are getting on with most of our daily work. To pray at all times also seems to be part of the spiritual armour of which Paul speaks in Ephesians 6; we can use tongues as protection, as a way of attack, to win and be victorious.

A most beautiful extension to the gift of speaking in tongues is singing in tongues, and there is great joy and release in singing out in a heavenly language which is pure praise to God. How wonderful, when the English words run out, to move on into singing in the Spirit and know that we are praising him fully as he deserves. We may find ourselves starting to sing in English, then changing to tongues, using the same tune. Or we may find the Spirit giving us a tune as well as words. Some people who speak in tongues have never yet experimented with singing in tongues, yet it opens up a whole new range of worship and praise to the Lord, and I find it an invaluable addition to my times of worship.

Many Christian song tapes and records include a time of singing in the Spirit, and one way of releasing our own language is to join in with such a tape. You will find the Lord giving you words and tune, and that they will blend in and harmonise beautifully with the recorded voices.

SHOUTING AND NOISE

Shout, verb. Make loud articulate or inarticulate cry or vocal sound, speak loudly.

Noise, noun. Loud outcry, clamour, shouting, din of voices and movements; any sound.

Psalm 132.9: Let thy saints shout for joy.

This is perhaps one reason why it is good to be alone with the Lord – and even better if the house is empty! Or maybe we can try this when we are out in a park or field and there is no one else around. Psalm 100 exhorts us to 'make a joyful noise to the Lord', and Psalm 89 says, 'Blessed are the people who know the festal shout'. The late David Watson used to encourage congregations to do this at meetings – to raise a great shout of praise to the Lord.

We shall probably all feel self-conscious even thinking

about shouting, let alone actually making a joyful noise. For us it may be hard enough just speaking out words of praise. Yet if the desire to praise the Lord is deep within us, and God so moves us, shouting can be a real release. As we see, it is certainly scriptural, so we need not be worried that we are doing something silly – but obviously there will be a right time and place for it for each individual Christian.

PRACTICAL

Choose one of the elements in this chapter and start using it in your quiet time. Do so as long as it takes you to feel it has become part of your praise and worship. Then go on to another element, and continue in this way. Keep a record of the way any one element changed or enhanced your quiet time, your feelings about it, etc.

PRAYER

Dear Lord, your word says that what comes out of the mouth originally starts in the heart, and this is what defiles a man (Matthew 15.18). Lord, I do desire that my heart shall be so cleansed and right with you that the thoughts of my mind and the words of my mouth will be pure and lovely. I ask that you will accept the praise and worship that I bring you with my mouth and lips and tongue, and that you will so enlarge my love for you that my times of vocal praise will lift me into your presence.   Amen.

NOTES

1   See Chapters 6,7 and 8.
2   1 Samuel 2.1; 2 Samuel 22; Luke 1.46 and Luke 1.67.
3   See chapter 8 on the Holy Spirit.
4   Jackie Pullinger, *Chasing the Dragon* (Hodder and Stoughton).

10

Using the Body in Worship

Although this chapter describes several ways of worshipping the Lord through the use of our bodies, we first have to look at what motivates such movement. If you have children, you will know that they often express their feelings in physical activity. The same is equally true for adults when we forget our inhibitions. We have only to look at the way spectators react when their favourite football team achieves the winning goal; their excitement and delight leads them to jump up and down, and wave their arms about, or clap each other heartily on the back, sometimes even to run on to the pitch! Emotions such as anger or hatred lead to a clenched fist and the raised arm. Many of us, too, know the temptation to smack a child when we are angry – physical movements which are motivated by inner feelings and emotions.

As our experience of the Lord deepens we shall discover that our emotions and feelings are touched. This was one of the things I found as I began to experiment with new ways of worshipping. Once, during a time of confession, I found myself in tears; another time I became aware that I was smiling in joy and wonder at something the Lord had shown me. Sometimes I've even found myself having a chuckle with the Lord, for our God likes to laugh with his people.

The areas of praise and worship that we have looked at will inevitably lead to the release of our feelings. You cannot spend five or ten minutes praising the Lord and not experience some moving in your heart! Many of us have been brought up to the belief that it is wrong to show or give way to our emotions. Or we are scared of showing any sign of weakness in this respect – we don't want other people to see us as we really are, and so we maintain the traditional British stiff upper lip! Fortunately, the Lord wants to be in every area of our lives; he knows that it is good for us to allow our emotions to come to the surface and not be suppressed, and how much better for them to do so in his company. The Lord wants us to show how we are really feeling; that we really are sorry for our wrongdoings, or that we really are happy to be with him.

Many of us know what it is like to feel the joy and nearness of the Lord when we are in church or at a special praise meeting. But we don't have to be with hundreds of other people to create the same atmosphere. Yet again we must remind ourselves that the Lord lives in the praise his people bring him, so it is only logical that we should use this method to bring us close to him so that our meetings together are vibrant and alive. We do not need to utilise all the aspects of worship mentioned here, but it is worth exploring them to see if they enhance our worship.

An army officer in our church congregation shared in a discussion how he had become aware of the Lord in a totally new way once he had begun to praise and worship him. He found, to his surprise, that during one of his quiet times he was actually sobbing before the Lord. Quite a testimony from a man with his military background.

Though we have no actual record of Jesus laughing or smiling, Hebrews 1.9 attributes to him the words of Psalm 45, that God 'anointed him with the oil of gladness', and he told his disciples to 'rejoice and leap for joy' (Luke 6.23). We also know the great love he has for us all, and love is just as much an emotion as the tears he wept at the grave of Lazarus.

There are many, many verses in Scripture which describe human emotions. Here are just a few:

Psalm 126.5:	'May those who sow in tears reap with shouts of joy!'
Psalm 126.2:	'Our mouth was filled with laughter, and our tongue with shouts of joy'.
Luke 7.38:	'She wet his feet with her tears'.
Ecclesiastes 3.4:	'A time to weep, and a time to laugh.'
Psalm 16.11:	'In thy presence there is fullness of joy'.
Psalm 34.6:	'This poor man cried, and the Lord heard him.'
Matthew 25.23:	'Enter into the joy of your master.'

Once our emotions are set free we shall soon discover release in other areas, not least in our bodies. Praising the Lord in physical ways is a natural progression from the vocal praise we bring him, and will often occur as we sing and worship the Lord.

LIFTING HANDS

Psalm 134.2: 'Lift up your hands to the holy place'. The lifting, or dropping, of our hands is symbolic of various inner attitudes. Raising our hands can be a symbol of supplication – the picture comes to mind of a harsh Victorian landlord just about to evict his tenants, while the latter are kneeling before him with hands raised in a plea for mercy.

The dropping of hands can imply weakness or a lack of resolution, hence the Bible's call to 'strengthen the weak hands' (Isaiah 35.3). This is pictured vividly in the story of Moses, who stood on a hill overlooking the children of Israel as they were in a battle with Amalek (Exodus 17.8–13). Every time Moses held up his hand, Israel prevailed; but when he lowered his hand, Amalek prevailed. But after a while his arms grew tired and heavy, so Aaron and Hur sat Moses down on a stone and each held up one of his hands till the sun set, and Israel won the battle. So the weak hands of Moses became God's symbol of victory.

The hand can also be a symbol of power, and when we

raise ours to God we are showing him that we deny our rights to our own power in order to glorify his. We are also showing him that we are denying our shyness and inhibitions in order to put him first. We may feel awkward about raising our hands in public, wondering what other people will think. One way round this is to shut our eyes! In fact, we may well find that our eyes will be shut anyway when we are praising the Lord, and our hands may rise naturally as we begin to feel his love with us and his presence surrounding us. In fact, this was the customary attitude for prayer in New Testament times and the early Christian teacher Origen wrote: 'The best position is to stand, with hands held out, even as you want to lift up your soul, and raise your mind to God'. If we can learn to raise our hands to the Lord in our quiet time, it will greatly lessen our feelings of inhibition if we want to use this expression of worship in church or at a meeting.

Like many of the elements explored in this book, raising our hands is an outward sign of an experience going on within our hearts. It is not something to do simply because other people do it, but because our hearts are motivating us within: 'Let us lift up our hearts and hands to God in heaven' (Lamentations 3.41).

CLAPPING

Psalm 47.1: 'Clap your hands, all peoples!'

This is one of the easiest forms of body worship, certainly in company with others. Ironically, it is often much harder to do on one's own! Generally we either clap in time to music that we are listening to, or in response to and appreciation of something we like. Clapping can likewise be our response to God, and often praise meetings spontaneously erupt in hearty clapping to the Lord just because of who he is.

Of course, if we clap while we are singing, it does need to be done sensibly and sensitively for it to enhance our worship. Some people thoughtlessly just clap loudly on each beat in a way that is distracting to others and takes away the sense of worship. In this respect it is a good idea to watch how others clap in your fellowship, to see if you can learn ways that will enhance the worship time.

KNEELING

Psalm 95.6: 'O come, let us worship and bow down, let us kneel before the Lord, our maker!'

Daniel 6.10: 'He got down upon his knees three times a day and prayed and gave thanks before his God.'

I grew up in a church where we had extremely good teaching and grounding in the word of God. Kneeling, however, was not part of the way we worshipped, so it was a totally new experience when we joined our present Anglican church after moving to a new area. Yet I have noticed that this tradition seems to be practised less than when we first joined, and very few people kneel in our services now. (There was much laughter at a recent Parochial Church Council meeting when it was pointed out that forty-eight hassocks were in urgent need of repair yet the number of people kneeling on them in the services could be counted on one hand!).

Kneeling before the Lord in our quiet times can be a moving experience. I find myself kneeling when I am really desperate about something I am praying for, or when I feel convicted of sin and need to confess. Kneeling is also an acknowledgement that we are in the presence of royalty, and there is no greater king than King Jesus. So kneeling is another outward sign showing what we feel in our hearts. It is also a recognition of Christ's lordship in our lives, and of the respect we want to bring him: 'At the name of Jesus every knee shall bow' (Philippians 2.10).

STANDING

Deuteronomy 10.8 '. . . to stand before the Lord to minister to him and to bless his name.'

Standing is also a sign of respect. This is seen in the way a congregation may stand as their vicar or minister takes his place, or a courtroom will stand at the entrance of the judge, or an audience may stand when the leader of an orchestra comes on stage, and even more strikingly in the 'standing ovations' often spontaneously given in praise of a specially good speech or performance. By standing in the Lord's presence we are acknowledging his sovereignty and Godhead as well as our love and respect for him. The verse from Deuteronomy quoted above really comes alive when we picture ourselves in our priestly role, ministering to the Lord and praising him as we stand in his presence. A similar verse in 2 Chronicles 29.11 tells us that the Lord has chosen us to stand before him. By asking us to stand, God is drawing us up to him. We do not have to stay in fear on our knees – though that is obviously a good starting position. God has restored us to a right relationship with him; in fact we are joint heirs with his son, Jesus (Romans 8.17). Therefore, because of what Jesus has done on the cross, we can stand upright before God and not be ashamed of what we are, but joyful that we are counted worthy to stand before him.

It can also be good to stand up simply as a way of renouncing any laziness or lethargy we may be feeling during our quiet time. We can, after all, sometimes get too comfortable in our chairs!

DANCING

2 Samuel 6.14: 'David danced before the Lord with all his might.'

It probably would not occur to many Christians to get up out of their seats and dance when they are alone with God. Those who have used this form of worship in their quiet times find it very releasing and a wonderful way of showing their love. For many (especially young) people, to 'dance for joy' is a natural way of expressing strong feelings of pleasure or thankfulness – and dancing is beginning to be used as an integral part of common worship in church in some parts of the world. People involved in such groups stress the importance of praying together as often as they practise together. When you are on your own, however, you might try liturgical dances to set steps, or just move and dance before the Lord as the Spirit leads you. You could try dancing to a record or tape, or else provide the music yourself as you sing and praise the Lord.

Physical praise and body worship is a natural response to the moving of the Holy Spirit in our lives as he releases our fears and inhibitions and as we allow him to touch our emotions.

PRACTICAL

1   Choose one of the aspects of worship in this chapter and practise using it in your quiet time. Then look for opportunities for using it in public worship.
2   Look up other biblical references to these five elements and discover more of how they were used.

PRAYER

Father, I ask that I will be so aware of your love in my life and your presence within me, that my body will freely respond to you, and that I will be released into worshipping you in this physical way.   Amen.

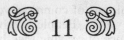

11

Prayer

An American survey estimated that the average minister spends only two minutes a day in prayer, and the average lay Christian only one minute. Yet Scripture shows us that prayer is a vital and necessary part of our spiritual lives. Prayer can be of three kinds. Firstly, there is prayer as an informal, intimate daily conversation with God, in which we share our thoughts and ideas, fears and worries; this can include praise and worship. Secondly, there is prayer in which we ask the Lord for specific things for ourselves; this is petitioning prayer. Thirdly, intercessory prayer is praying on behalf of others, at times including those who cannot or will not pray for themselves.

All three categories can form part of our own personal devotions or quiet time, as well as being part of the wider context of church meetings (particularly prayers of intercession). It is very important to spend time regularly talking and chatting with God, and to feel completely at ease with him as we share our everyday life. It would be rather rude, to say the least, to ignore God for days, then suddenly come to him when something goes wrong and expect him to listen and answer just like that! So prayer is first of all being honest and natural with God, chatting to him in our minds or aloud during our quiet times, or indeed at other times during the day. God knows the thoughts and intentions of our hearts already, so we don't have to produce empty, meaningless phrases, or use long words as the Pharisee did (Luke 18.10–12); the cry of our soul is enough.

Petitioning prayer is going one stage further, and asking

the Lord for specific things in our lives. Jesus taught his disciples the prayer we know as the Lord's Prayer. This covers many areas of our daily needs: food, clothing, housing and so on. Petitioning prayer can also be a time for examining ourselves, to make sure that our requests are not selfish or wrong. Indeed, some people do not like to ask God for things for themselves. They feel that God has not got time to be bothered with their desires or needs, and that it is selfish to expect him to do so. But this limits our God, and our expectations of him. If we have this attitude we are in danger of making our God seem small when in fact he is immeasurably big – and all-seeing, all-knowing, all-powerful, present everywhere and available to everyone. God may in fact answer a selfish prayer in order to encourage us to trust him, though this will probably only be in the early stages of our Christian walk. I can remember that as a young child I had locked the door of our lounge because I was frightened of burglars! Then I heard my father trying to open the door, but the key had somehow jammed in the lock. I lay in bed upstairs and prayed that God would open the door, and after a short time I heard the key turn and the door open. I was greatly encouraged at the time, and it helped me to trust the Lord for answers to other prayers.

The Bible has many examples of people who prayed prayers for themselves, and indeed some of them show that these seemingly selfish prayers actually fitted in with God's wider desire and plan for either their lives or those of other people.

The story of Hannah is one example. We read in 1 Samuel chapter 1 how she was desperate for a child, and 'poured out her soul before the Lord'. Her prayer was answered, and she gave birth to a boy whom she called Samuel. This child experienced the Lord at an early age, and later proved to be a great blessing to his country as the Lord established him as a prophet in Israel (1 Samuel 3.20). The whole country was blessed – all because a woman prayed for a baby!

In 2 Kings chapter 20, we read the story of Hezekiah, who was so ill that he actually lay dying on his bed. He was told by the prophet Isaiah that he would soon die, and so he turned his face to the wall, prayed, and wept bitterly. Before Isaiah had time to leave the palace, God told him to go back and tell Hezekiah that his prayer was answered and that fifteen years would be added to his life. We are then told later on (2 Chronicles 30) how God used Hezekiah to reinstate the passover feast and to pray for the people: 'They took confidence because of Hezekiah', says chapter 32.8 – and all because of a seemingly selfish prayer.

So petitioning for ourselves often fits in with God's plan, either for our own lives, or his wider plan for others. But we need not confine such prayers to practical things or daily needs. We can use this time to ask God to enter more and more into the deep areas of our lives; like healing past hurts, opening up new aspects of our personalities, or revealing ways in which we may be displeasing him. This is also the time to seek his will regarding our future, our jobs, marriage prospects, or anything else which may concern us.

Intercession is the word used to describe our prayers for other people, situations or the world. Here we need to beware of falling into the trap of being too casual in our intercessory prayers. It is very easy to think of someone and just say: 'Dear Lord, please bless so and so.' Real intercession is hard work, and will involve the sacrifice of much time and effort, partly because we need to think carefully about the individual or situation, and be specific as we ask the Lord to enter in. Intercession cannot be done in one or two minutes. A good period of time needs to be set aside, and we shall only do this if we are really motivated to prayer.

In the Bible itself we find prayer referred to as a sacrifice: 'Let my prayer be counted as incense before thee, and the lifting up of my hands as an evening sacrifice' (Psalm 141.2). It is interesting to note how prayer is often mentioned in relation to incense – which was part of the sacrificial offering to God in Old Testament times. In other words, prayer is an offering to God, and you only offer to him what is valuable to you and what you are willing to give up. In Luke 1.9.10 we read: 'It fell by lot to Zechariah to enter the temple of the Lord and burn incense, and the whole multitude of the people were praying outside at the hour of incense.' And Revelation 5.8 speaks of 'golden bowls of incense, which are the prayers of the saints.' When we come to interceding for others, we must be willing to sacrifice ourselves by setting time aside, and using such prayer as an offering to God.

The Bible records a great many prayers of different people, and it is interesting to study the varied forms their prayers took and how they approached the Lord. One vivid description of intercession can be found in Job 16.21 (AV): 'O that one might *plead* for a man with God, as a man pleadeth for his neighbour.' Elsewhere God himself is shown as seeing this time of intercession as a coming together – of him and us – to argue a cause or case: 'Come now, let us reason together, says the Lord' (Isaiah 1.18). Job used a similar argument in chapter 23 when he said: 'I would lay my case before him and fill my mouth with arguments . . . There an upright man could reason with him.'

If we want an example of how to plead a cause before the Lord we have only to look in Genesis chapter 18. God decides to tell Abraham that he is going to destroy the cities of Sodom and Gomorrah, and when he does so, Abraham starts to plead for the lives of the people. He uses God's own love of justice for individuals to plead the cause of many, and tells God it would not be in his nature to do such a thing. In fact, he says, it would go against one of God's main characteristics – that of being just!

Similarly, when God was angry at the Israelites and wanted to punish them, Moses 'besought the Lord' (Exodus 32.11), and argued with him along the lines of: 'What will the Egyptians say when they hear this?' He also reminded God of his former promises to bless and multiply the descendants of Abraham, Isaac and Jacob, and we read that 'the Lord repented of the evil which he thought to do to his people.'

So, studying the prayers of people in Scripture can give us hints and clues as to the way we can go about pleading the cause of the people for whom we are interceding.

But intercession is not just a case of sacrificial prayer, pleadings, cries or beseechings. We find, in Colossians 4.2, that Paul has three very helpful points to make regarding our prayers for other people, or for ourselves. First he shows the need to continue in prayer and not to give up. It is very easy to give up if we don't feel that the Lord is working or answering our prayers. In situations like these it is particularly helpful to have other Christians to encourage us and share the burden of long-term intercession.

The second helpful point that Paul makes concerns being watchful. We should actually be on the look-out for signs that the Lord is working. Some years ago Peter hurt his back rather badly, and we asked three friends to come over and pray with him. To begin with he was stretched out on the floor unable to get up. We began to pray, and after a while asked him if there was any sign of improvement. There was just a little, so we took encouragement from this and carried on praying. Again we asked if there was anything happening, and this time he was able to move a bit more. So we carried on praying and watching for more signs, and within an hour or so he was able to stand up and sit down normally, suffering only from slight soreness. We learned a valuable lesson that day about being watchful.

The third point is that we must be thankful. This is not just tagged on to the end of the verse as an afterthought, but meant to be an integral part of our prayers as we continue steadfast and watchful. Most of the New Testament references to prayer are closely linked with thanksgiving: 'In everything, by prayer and supplication, with thanksgiving let your requests be made known to God,' says Paul again (Philippians 4.6). This is where we can develop a new attitude to intercession. We may start with the pleadings and supplication, but we must be aware that our initial prayers have already set the power of God moving. Therefore, to continue to plead is in fact to ask God to do something he has already begun. In the example of Peter's back, we began by asking the Lord to help and heal, and continued to do so without giving up. Then we began looking for signs of God's working, 'being watchful' for any improvement, at the same time thanking God for a small beginning and continuing to thank him for what he was going to do.

Once our prayers change from constant begging to being full of thanks, we shall experience a marked growth in our level of faith, all the more important when we remember that it is 'the prayer of faith' that 'will save the sick man' (James 5.15).

One way to increase our faith when praying is to use 'visioning prayer'. This involves having a picture of the desired objective in our minds and keeping it before us as we pray. It really involves a radical change from praying negatively to praying positively. If we pray for someone's salvation, yet still see them in our minds eye as far away from the Lord as ever, we are putting a block on our faith. Visioning prayer means that we see that person in our mind as already a Christian, perhaps imagining them in church, worshipping and praising God. Thanking the Lord in advance also forms an important part of this type of prayer.

I first learnt about visioning prayer from the books by Agnes Sandford, and it brought about quite a change in my own prayer life. I remember trying to follow her example of visioning a prayer request when I heard a baby crying in the flats at the end of our garden. Instead of just asking the Lord to stop the child crying, I began to picture it snuggled up against its mother's breast, happy and contented. This was quite difficult to do at first, especially when I could still hear the cries! But I persevered, and after a couple of minutes the child quietened down. The same thing happened on two subsequent nights; each time the baby cried, I pictured it happy and contented and prayed and thanked accordingly. Each time, the Lord answered very quickly. Then it was that I noticed my faith and expectancy were considerably raised by this new prayer experience.

There may be times when we don't know exactly how to pray for people or situations. This is where it can be helpful to pray in tongues. We can get right to the heart of matters, because it is the Holy Spirit, joined with our spirits, who is speaking directly to God. This is done as we focus our minds on the person or situation concerned and then begin speaking in tongues. We may start by telling the Lord that we don't know how to pray, and asking the Holy Spirit to pray through us. This way there is no excuse for not knowing what to pray, for we can still be the channel through whom God works.

So when we are at a loss for words – the Holy Spirit certainly is not! For, we are told, 'the Spirit helps us in our weakness; for we do not know how to pray as we ought, but the Spirit himself intercedes for us with sighs too deep for words. And he who searches the hearts of men knows what is the mind of the Spirit, because the Spirit intercedes for the saints according to the will of God.' (Romans 8.26–7).

Like most Christians, I find it helpful to have a prayer list, which is constantly being changed and updated. I keep a note of the prayers and then write down the answers as and when they come. Keeping a record of the answers is a great encouragement to our faith, and inspires us to go on praying and asking the Lord for even greater things, and so widening the boundaries of our expectations.

But we all have to admit that there are times when our prayers do not seem to receive an answer; and obviously we wonder why this should be so. There may be several reasons. First, we need to be aware that the devil will try anything to stop us from praying, and we may need consciously to bind him and loose the person for whom we are praying (Matthew 16.19).[1] We need to be aware of the powerful forces of darkness (Ephesians 6.12) as portrayed in the story of Daniel (10.12–14). Here we see that the angel of God was held back by a prince of Satan for three weeks. This is yet another reason for being constant and watchful in prayer.

Another reason for unanswered prayer may be that we have been asking for the wrong thing, as we are warned in James 4.3: 'You ask and do not receive, because you ask wrongly, to spend it on your own passions.' Or our praying may be prompted by wrong motives, or by a sense of self-righteousness, as in the story of the Pharisee and the tax-collector (Luke 18).

Finally we have to ask ourselves if we are truly praying in accord with God's will – if not, we could be spending a lot of time praying, and yet wasting our breath! The passage from Romans 8 quoted above says that the Holy Spirit intercedes for the saints 'according to the will of God'. Because the Holy Spirit knows what is on God's heart, and knows his intentions, he is able to pray exactly in the Father's will. There may be circumstances that we know nothing about which are preventing God from working – perhaps some sin on the part of the other person. Jeremiah was told by God that because the people of Judah refused to mend their ways or change their lives, he was not to pray or intercede for them, for God would not listen! (Jeremiah 7.16). Or, the time may not be right even though the prayer request is valid.

As we sum up these thoughts on prayer, let us remember that the ears of the Lord are open to the prayers of the righteous, and that such prayers have great power in their effect (1 Peter 3.12, and James 5.16).

FASTING

Fast, verb. Abstain from all or some kinds of food as religious observance or in sign of mourning.

Ezra 8.23: We fasted and besought our God and he listened.

Fasting in conjunction with intercession is one way of showing God that we are really serious about our prayer requests. If we care enough for people, we shall willingly go without a meal to give more time to prayer. One elderly lady mentioned in the New Testament sets us such an example: 'She did not depart from the temple, worshipping with fasting and prayer night and day' (Luke 2.37).

Peter and I once belonged to a fellowship group where we had an agreement that whenever one of the wives became pregnant, we would all pray and fast. We tried to miss the same meal if possible, or at least to fast on the same day. The woman concerned was then very conscious of the selfless love and care of the members of the group, and each participant found fasting a valuable aid in their prayer life. If you are not used to fasting, its certainly helpful to start doing it with a group of others with the same prayer objective. It is never something to be entered into lightly, but only after first seeking God's will.

It is also very important to prepare your body beforehand, especially if you plan to fast for a whole day or more. When Peter and I first fasted for three days, we ate only raw vegetables and fruit the day preceding, and the day following the fast. Unfortunately, we neglected to do anything about tea and coffee, and when we cut these drinks out we ended up with terrible headaches the first evening, suffering the effects of withdrawal from the caffeine and tannin.

Fasting is definitely not something to rush into; it needs prayer, planning, and thought beforehand. But those who do fast testify to blessings received, prayers answered, and a deeper sense of fellowship with the Lord.

PRACTICAL

1   Ask yourself how much time you spend in prayer, and try adding five extra minutes for each type of prayer.
2   Buy a notebook to keep a record of your prayer requests. Mark off one side for the petitions, and the other side for the answers. Keep a note, too, of dates,

circumstances and other relevant details of the prayer.

3 Look up Exodus 32.11 for another example of how to plead before God.

PRAYER

Father, it amazes me that I can talk with you, the great and mighty God. Thank you that you delight in my prayers and are far more willing to hear and answer than I am to pray. Please increase and widen the boundaries of my faith as I see you answering my prayers in the coming days.   Amen.

NOTE

1 See chapter 15 on dealing with hindrances.

𝕸 12 𝕸

Reading God's Word

A major part of our quiet time will centre around the Bible. Christians throughout the ages have proved the power of the word of God, and if we immerse ourselves in the Bible, all through our lives we will experience the effect it has on our relationship with God and every aspect of life. Jesus quoted from the Scriptures many times during his ministry, not least to rebuke the devil and resist his temptations. The Word of God is not dead and empty words on a page, but is alive and active, and is able to pierce through the outer layers of our minds, and through our arguments and questions, to reveal the important issues of life (Hebrews 4.12). In Paul's picture of the armour of God, in Ephesians 6, it is the Word, the sword of the Spirit, which is the attacking weapon: we cannot fight in God's battle line if we are inadequately armed. Through the Bible we learn more of God, and are built up in our Christian lives. This is one of the major ways in which God speaks to his people. Paul urged the believers in Colossae to 'let the word of Christ dwell in you richly' (Colossians 3.16). The power of the Word of God is eternal: it can never be stopped or hindered and will last for ever (Isaiah 40.8 and Luke 21.33).

A good way of starting your time of Bible reading, and one used by many Christians, is to pray the words of Psalm 119.18: 'Open my eyes, that I may behold wondrous things out of thy law.' Because the Scriptures are God's word to us, it is important that we attentively receive his opening of them to us, and helping us to understand them and appropriate them in a personal way.

From the Hebrews of the Old Testament to the New Testament Church, God's people have placed the highest importance on the Word of God. Joshua 'read all the words of the law to the people', so that they would know how to live (Joshua 8.34). Paul exhorted his young friend Timothy to 'attend to the public reading of Scripture' (1 Timothy 4.13), and encouraged him to continue the good habit of reading God's word which started in his childhood, probably through the influence of his mother and grandmother (2 Timothy 3.14; 1.5).

As I suggested at the beginning of this book, a new Christian who has decided to read the Word of God seriously may well start to read the Bible like any other book – that is, by beginning at the beginning, and then reading on chapter by chapter. This is not a good idea. Much of the Old Testament is difficult to understand without some background explanation. To start with, new Christians may find it more helpful to read about the life of Christ in the Gospels, or perhaps something of the early Church in Acts. The 'Epistles' – the letters of Paul, Peter, James and John – are full of teaching on how to live the Christian life. But we must not be tempted to neglect the Old Testament entirely, especially when we remember that it was the only Scripture available to Jesus and to the early Christians; and they set us a good example of how to use the word of God.

It is advisable, therefore, to read the Bible within the framework of a plan. As a child I was given a little leaflet which listed all the chapters of the Bible with a little square for each chapter. They did not follow the Bible order, so that one week I might be reading a group of Psalms, and the following week something on the life of Christ. As I filled in each little square I was able to see the progress I made during the year. By alternating our reading of the Old and New Testaments in this way our interest will be constantly stimulated and we shall gain a valuable overall picture of Scripture. A similar leaflet is still available, as are several

Bible reading courses, like that produced by CWR which is laid out in such a way that the reader covers the whole Bible in one year.

The Bible can be read in many ways, and its full riches are not revealed unless we approach it on different levels.

STUDYING

Study, verb. Take pains to investigate or acquire knowledge of (subject).

2 Timothy 2.15(AV): Study . . . rightly dividing the word of truth.

Studying Scripture in depth should form part of every Christian's life. The dictionary definition shows that study requires some effort and discipline on our part. Though we have the promise of the Holy Spirit to 'bring all things to our remembrance,' (John 14.26), he cannot work in a vacuum. If we have never read, studied or learned the word of God in the first place, then the Holy Spirit cannot remind us of it months or years later when we need it. The Bible is God's living word to us, and the more we know and understand it, then the more in turn shall we understand our Lord, his character, his personality, and his dealings with us – his Church. Studying the Bible inevitably leads to a build-up of our faith, for we learn to trust God more in our daily lives when we see how faithful he is to his people in the Bible.

There are a great many Bible study aids on the market today, aimed at different ages and levels, so that we can all be helped in this important aspect of our quiet time. It can be helpful, too, to vary the way in which one studies. We may follow a system of notes for a few months, then change to studying a whole book of the Bible, or a character. The advantage of having daily notes is that they do help us to be disciplined in reading our Bibles each day; but on the other hand they can make us lazy. After all, it is someone else who has done the actual studying and work. It can be far more satisfying to follow through a theme or a book for ourselves. It is really exciting and rewarding to hunt through different cross-references, checking with concordances and dictionaries, and so to allow the Lord to speak directly to our minds and hearts.

A very helpful book to read on the question of studying the Bible is *Ye Search the Scriptures*, by the Chinese Christian, Watchman Nee.[1] He gives several practical suggestions on how and what to study. He makes the point that much time needs to be allocated to making ourselves acquainted with Scripture – and he talks in terms of hours, not minutes! Though it might be difficult for most of us to spend an hour or two in study each day, it would not be impossible to set aside one or two hours a week to devote to more serious study, while continuing of course a daily reading in our quiet time. Here is where the unemployed or housebound can use their extra leisure hours to good advantage.

Watchman Nee lists twenty-eight different plans for studying the Bible, ranging from principal persons, types and topics, through to chronology, miracles, prayers and terminology. Because all Scripture is inspired by God, it means that everything in it is of value to the Christian. There are even meanings attached to each different number mentioned in the Bible (for example, seven is the number of perfection).

The more time I spend in studying the Bible, the more it has become a real delight to me. As I read, a word or phrase will stand out and send me searching through different references, or hunting through my concordance. Sometimes I have found I had several ideas floating round my mind at once, so I have had to make a note of them in order to study them further at a later date. When this happened I found myself quite excited, and eager to continue my studies another day.

MEDITATION

Meditate, verb. Plan mentally, design; exercise the mind in (esp.

97

religious) contemplation (*on* subject) in order that the soul may increase in love of God and holiness of life.

Psalm 1.2 On his law he meditates day and night.

The practice of Bible meditation may be alien to many of us; this could be due in part to the insufficient time we set aside to spend with God. Yet it can be deeply satisfying to our souls and spirits to ponder slowly the words of a verse, or a phrase of Scripture. Meditation is yet another way in which we can take the word of God deep into our lives. It simply involves taking a verse, or a few words, or even just one word, and thinking deeply and prayerfully about it, examining it from every angle, looking for different nuances and meanings – saying it over to ourselves many times so that the full meaning sinks deep into our souls. Once I was reading Hebrews chapter 3, and found that the words 'holy brethren' stood out. Just two words, which became very precious to me as I thought for many days, on and off, about what they really meant, and my heart filled with love and gratefulness to the Lord as I began to realise that I, too, was holy.

A friend once described to me how she had spent many months studying and meditating on the Song of Solomon, taking just one verse, or as small a portion as suited the context. She found it very rewarding slowly and carefully to meditate on such a small portion. She made notes as she went along, and found the book 'absolutely fabulous' as she put it!

David, in Psalm 34.8 describes meditation in the words: 'O taste and see that the Lord is good!' We get the picture here of someone taking the words of Scripture and eating them, chewing them over slowly and digesting them. We take them deep into ourselves; and the word of God, which is powerful, living and active, does a work of healing, restoration and love in our lives which we may not even be aware of at the time, but whose effects remain with us all our life.

MEMORISING

Memorise, verb. Put on record; commit to memory.

Psalm 119.11: I have laid up thy word in my heart that I might not sin against thee.

The practice of memorising scripture seems to have declined in recent years. To help us in this area, some organisations, like the Navigators, supply cards printed with different texts to learn. The idea is that it's easier to carry a small pack of cards around in your handbag or pocket than a large Bible! The Christian can then utilise odd moments during the day, such as waiting for a bus or train, to memorise a verse at a time, using the cards as an aid.

Another aid to remembering Scripture is to underline or otherwise mark some verses in your Bible so that your eyes are drawn to them. Or you can write the verses out yourself, to imprint them on your mind, like taking notes for an exam. Or you may find it helpful to recite a verse or verses over and over again, thinking about them carefully and visualising the words in your mind as you speak them out.

Whatever method we use, it is important to memorise Scripture so that it becomes a living part of ourselves. It will also give us a store of Scripture for those times when for one reason or another we may not be able to read our Bibles. After the trauma of a divorce, a friend found that she could not retain anything she read, apart from the Bible. Her vicar gave her a book on meditation which suggested memorising verses and portions of Scripture, and she spent nine months meditating and memorising different parts of the Bible. Later on, she developed diabetes and almost totally lost her sight. During many months of trying to come to terms with her new illness, when she was unable to read, it was the remembered word of God that kept her going and gave her faith and peace. Now, with her sight fully restored and her diabetes stabilised, she can look back and see why it was necessary for her to learn so much Scripture.

Bible knowledge will not come to us overnight. We need carefully to read, study, meditate and memorise it for it to be of real and lasting value to us. In addition, the more Scripture we know, the more we shall be able to answer those who question us. On a visit to Thessalonica (Acts 17) Paul 'argued with them for three weeks from the scriptures, explaining and proving that it was necessary for the Christ to suffer and to rise from the dead . . .' Some of the people were persuaded to believe but because some were jealous (verse 5), Paul and Silas were hounded out. They went to Beroea and here the Jews 'received the word with all eagerness, examining the Scriptures daily to see if these things were so', and 'many of them therefore believed'. Paul would not have been so instrumental in bringing so many people to the Lord had he not been thoroughly grounded in Scripture.

So we, if we want to be of use to God and be equipped for his work, must take pains to study and learn all we can, for 'All scripture is inspired by God, and is profitable for teaching, for reproof, for correction and for training in righteousness' (2 Timothy 3.16).

PRACTICAL

1   Make a study of Psalm 119, noting how many times reference is made to the word of God, and how it affected the life of the writer. Apply each verse to your own situation.

2   Check in your concordance, and through cross-references, the number of characteristics applied to the word of God – I have found well over twenty!

3   Make a plan for yourself of what portions of Scripture you would like to study. Decide when you can set time aside for in-depth research – perhaps one evening a week. Also think about making a definite decision to read the

Bible through in one year. (This can be achieved by reading three chapters a day and five on Sunday!)

PRAYER

Thank you, Father, for the privilege of reading your word. Please fill me with zeal and eagerness to study and learn it, so that it does indeed become active in my life.   Amen.

SOME PUBLISHERS OF BIBLE READING NOTES

The Bible Society, *Bible Reading Plan.*
The Bible Reading Fellowship. *Daylight, Guidelines.*
Bible Today Ltd, *Listening to God* (based on individual books of the Bible).
Crusade for World Revival, *Every Day with Jesus*
The Salvation Army/Hodder and Stoughton, *The Soldier's Armoury*
Scripture Union, *Daily Bread, Daily notes, Alive to God*
St Andrew Press, *The Upper Room*

NOTE

1   Watchman Nee, *Ye Search the Scriptures* (Christian Fellowship, New York).

13

Hearing God Speak in Natural Ways

In this chapter we shall look at some of the things we can do to make it easier for us to hear God, and how some of the attitudes of our hearts and minds may affect our ability to hear him speaking to us. We shall also see some of the more natural and everyday ways that God uses to speak to his people.

You may well ask, especially if you are a new Christian, how exactly do you hear from God? This whole concept of hearing God speak can be quite a mystery to some Christians. They may expect, at first, to hear an actual voice, and may feel guilty, hurt or disappointed when this doesn't happen. The situation is sometimes unintentionally made worse by the testimony of other Christians who seem to say glibly, 'The Lord spoke to me . . .' It may make new believers question the fact – God doesn't seem to speak to them.

Of course the Lord does speak to each of his people, but we have to be on the right wavelength, and in tune with him. This is one reason why our quiet times are so important; for by simply spending time with God, getting to know him better, and praising and worshipping him, we are putting ourselves in the right position to hear him. He will speak directly and personally to us if we are available and listening. Jeremiah experienced this in the most unpromising circumstances. He was 'shut up in the court of the guard' when God spoke to him, saying: 'Call to me, and I will answer you, and will tell you great and hidden things which you have not known' (Jeremiah 33.3). This is a tremendous promise.

If the Lord has invited us into his presence then it is because he has something to say. So if we start off by realising that God is far more willing to speak to us than we are to listen, then we are in a good position to hear his 'still small voice'.

As Christians, we have the marvellous privilege of entering into the presence of God. This was not so before Jesus came. In Deuteronomy chapter 5 we read how the Israelites were afraid to go near the mountain where God was, in case the fire of God consumed them. They called on Moses to be their intermediary and to speak and listen to God on their behalf. All through the Old Testament the Jews could only approach God through the intermediary of a priest, or someone especially appointed by God. Now, Jesus, our great high priest, is seated at the right hand of God for ever interceding for us (Hebrews 7.25). Through him we now have free and immediate access to the throne room (Hebrews 10. 19–20). So there is no longer any need for us to be afraid of God, or to go through any human intermediary. He is ready to hear us and to speak to us right where we are – now!

To be receptive to his voice, and expectant of hearing him, it will help if we cultivate the two attitudes of listening and waiting.

LISTENING

Listen, verb. Make effort to hear something, hear person speaking with attention; give ear to.

Psalm 81.13: 'O that my people would listen to me.'

It is helpful if we are comfortable while we prepare to listen to the Lord. If our bodies are too tense, or we are too cold, or too hot, or our back aches because the chair is uncomfortable, our minds will keep coming back to our physical discomforts, instead of relaxing and thinking of the Lord. It can be a great blessing, as well, to sit quietly in his presence, not thinking about anything in particular, not wanting anything from him, but just to enjoy his company. That was the testimony of an older lady who told how she would often wake up in the middle of the night and spend an hour or so with God, just enjoying being with him. I felt that my own increasing awareness of the Lord was rather small and insignificant beside her powerful testimony!

Some people find that God speaks to them while they are on the move. Another friend shared that she heard the Lord many times while taking her dog for a walk. For myself, it was while I was hoovering that he put into my mind the idea of writing down these thoughts! And from Scripture we have the story of the two disciples walking on the Emmaus road, who said afterwards: 'Did not our hearts burn within us while he talked to us on the road?' (Luke 24.32). God is not limited by any conditions that we lay down; so we need to widen our thinking and expect him to speak to us at any time, in any place. However, this is far more likely to happen when we have already spent time cultivating the two-way relationship in our quiet time.

If we really want to hear from God, we have persistently to put ourselves in the situation where he can speak to us. I have suggested that for most of us that will almost certainly involve our daily quiet time. Here it may be worth reading again the section on right preparation in chapter 5, and especially the aspects of confession and forgiveness. It is important that there should be a clear channel between us and the Lord, unblocked by any sinful attitudes on our part. Another thing to remember is that God will speak to us – or we will hear his voice – only if he knows that we are not only waiting expectantly, but are prepared to do what he says – in other words, if he knows that we will be obedient.

Jesus once told his listeners that the reason they could not understand what he was saying was because they could not bear to hear his word. And the reason for that was because they had no will to obey the desires of God – only the desires of their father, the devil (John 8.43–4). Strong language, to people who prided themselves on being God's chosen people!

There is a beautiful picture of obedience in Exodus 21. The Jewish law laid down that every Hebrew slave was to be set free after serving his master for six years. But if, at the end of that time, he said, 'I love my master . . . I will not go free,' then his master was to pierce his ear as a sign that he was voluntarily bound to him for life. It is surely significant that it was the slave's *ear* that was to be pierced, for a slave cannot serve and obey his master unless he first *hears* his commands. It also illustrates the fact that obedience may be painful and costly!

Another reason why we may not hear God is that we are very often too busy talking ourselves, and don't give him the opportunity to speak. Or, if we don't really believe the Lord will speak to us, then we shall probably not even get to the stage of asking, as the boy Samuel did: 'Speak, Lord, for thy servant hears.'

But when we are convinced of God's desire to share his thoughts with us, our natural response will be to say: 'What do you want to say to me today Lord?' or, 'Have you a word for me in this or that situation?'

WAITING

Wait, verb. 1. Abstain from action or departure till some expected event occurs; pause, tarry, stay, be expectant or on the watch. 2. Act as waiter, as servant, as attendant.

Habakkuk 2.3: If it (the vision) seems slow, wait for it.

Isaiah 64.4: No eye has seen a God beside thee, who works for those who wait for him.

We see from the dictionary that there are two main meanings to this word: either to abstain from action, or to act as a waiter or servant. The former is something most of us find it hard to do. We are impatient by nature and want instant

105

results and immediate answers. We want God to act straight away, and are rarely prepared just to sit quietly. Especially we find silence difficult to cope with; most of us have experienced this in a public prayer meeting, where people seem awkward and fidgety if there is silence for any length of time. Yet these are the moments when God is likely to speak – in the silence – if we are alert and expecting him to do so. Similarly, in our personal devotions we need not be wary of times of silence, but see them as part of our overall worship. 'It is good that one should wait quietly for the salvation of the Lord' (Lamentations 3.26).

Many of us find it hard to sit still and wait. With maybe a short time at our disposal, we feel the pressure of our prayer list, or the neighbour who needs visiting, or the talk that needs preparing. But this is the time to put God first, and to sit and wait until he speaks. We need expectant hearts, believing that he *will* speak. Are we prepared to stay in his presence until he does? I am reminded of Jacob's prayer: 'I will not let you go, unless you bless me' (Genesis 32.26). Dare we say to the Lord, 'I will not leave this room till you speak to me?' Honest questions and expectant hearts will call forth a response from the living God.

We also find it hard to wait for the answers to prayers. Again we need to exercise patience. 'Be still before the Lord, and wait patiently for him,' says the Psalmist (Psalm 37.7).

When we don't get immediate results to our prayers, we may wonder if God has really heard us; or is he simply doing nothing about answering us? The passage in Daniel 10 referred to in the chapter on Prayer is very revealing in this matter, for it shows the forces of evil which are continually trying to counteract the prayers of God's people. This is one of the reasons why we need to persist in prayer and in waiting for the answer.

The second dictionary definition is that of waiting upon someone as a servant or attendant, and of purposely keeping close behind them. This came vividly to life to me in the television coverage of the tour of Australia by the Prince and Princess of Wales in 1983. When they were climbing Ayers Rock, another woman could be seen walking closely behind the Princess, and I realised she must have been the lady-in-waiting. This is just what God wants us to be – men and women in waiting, close behind and close enough to hear him when he speaks to us. Close enough, therefore, to serve him. Close enough to wait upon him. And what a privilege there is in being so close to Royalty, for where they go – we go! This privilege is ours as we wait upon the King of kings. Who knows where he will lead if we are close enough to hear what he says?

Having examined our own attitudes, we can now look at some of the natural ways in which God chooses to speak to us. God is not limited in the way he speaks to his people. His methods are numerous and varied, and he uses both natural, or human or earthly, channels, and divine or supernatural channels.

It is to the Bible that our thoughts turn first, for here we have God's own words direct to his people. The whole of Scripture is God's revealed word to his people, and he is able to use it to feed, guide, direct, admonish, comfort, teach and help us. But there are times when a particular verse or passage will have a special significance for us, and we find him speaking directly to our hearts. I experienced this the night before my parents separated and my mother and I went to live in a bed-sitter together. I was reading my Bible, when my eyes were drawn to Isaiah 66.13: 'As one whom his mother comforts, so I will comfort you.' God's protective love really came home to me as I read those words, and they were a great strength to me in the following months. We may read a particular chapter or verse many, many times in the course of our studies, but it is really thrilling when God uses such a general word to speak to us in a particular way to meet a specific need.

The way in which we hear from God is very much a

personal matter. Some people testify to a small, inner voice 'speaking' to them. Sceptics may describe this as our conscience – but why should not God use our conscience as a way of getting through to us? A few people seem to have the joy of hearing an actual voice, speaking aloud. This was the wonderful experience of a mature Christian woman, whose joy was doubled by the discovery that at the time the Lord spoke to her, he was also speaking to her husband; they were able to compare notes later.

For most of us, though, it would seem to be a matter of gaining confidence through the thoughts that come to us as we listen and wait, believing, as Scripture says, that 'we have the mind of Christ' (1 Corinthians 2.16). Just as we have to use our tongues, mouths and vocal cords when we speak in tongues, so we begin to realise that, if God is going to give us his thoughts, then he will have to use our minds to put his thoughts into. Then we shall discover with the Psalmist, 'how precious to me are thy thoughts' (Psalm 139.17).

God may also use other Christians as his mouthpiece, particularly over the matter of guidance, which may come to us through a more mature Christian in our fellowship, our pastor, vicar or elder. He may use some Christian book or article to make his thoughts and will known to us. We do, however, need to be very careful who we take advice from, and not go hopping from one person to another till we get the advice that fits in with our own plans! This is where it is important to check one form of communication with another. It would be folly to accept the advice of another person if it was totally opposed to biblical teaching.

Apart from our quiet times, we can also expect God to speak to us as we meet and worship with other Christians, especially during the services at our church or place of worship. Here again, we need to go in an expectant frame of mind, anticipating that God will communicate with us. People with families may find it particularly difficult getting to church relaxed and in tune with the Lord after feeding and clothing the children and preparing a Sunday dinner. It helps greatly, though, if we take a few minutes beforehand to think about the coming service and ask the Lord to prepare our hearts to receive a word from him. We can be in the same attitude of mind as we sit in church waiting for the service to begin, praying for ourselves and for those around us, that the Holy Spirit will be moving upon the fellowship, preparing us to receive the word.

God may speak to us at any time during the service. Perhaps through a hymn, a Bible reading, a prayer, or of course the teaching time in the sermon or talk. I'm sure many of us have experienced an occasion when we felt the preacher or speaker was speaking directly to us, as if he knew what we needed to hear that day; but of course we knew it was the Lord using that particular person.

To summarise, we can be sure that as we prepare ourselves and wait in an attitude of expectancy, the Lord will make his thoughts and will known to us, and our quiet times will be full of dialogue between the Lord and ourselves.

PRACTICAL

Start by sitting quietly for two or three minutes each day and ask the Lord to speak directly to you. Keep a note of your thoughts and any ideas, or words of Scripture that may come into your mind. Also be on the look-out all day and every day for God to speak to you.

PRAYER

Father, I thank you that you want to say so much to me, and share your thoughts ideas and plans. I look forward eagerly for what you are going to say to me today. Thank you.
Amen.

14

Hearing God Speak in Supernatural Ways

As God moves his worldwide Church forward in the things of the Spirit, we find him using what may seem to us to be unusual and supernatural ways to speak to his people. If we are aware of these different ways and are expecting God to use them, then we are in a far better position to recognise his voice.

There are two ways of viewing life. We can believe that we live only in the here and now, and that reality is only what we know, or can see or hear. We are in a sort of time box, and nothing exists outside of it; we are limited to our five senses. Or we can believe what the Bible teaches, that there is a spiritual realm running parallel with this physical realm. Christians know that we have entered a new kingdom – the Kingdom of Heaven – which is a spiritual kingdom, where we seek to walk in the Spirit and not in the flesh (Galatians 5.16). Some earlier cultures, like those of American Indians or the ancient Greeks, found it easier to accept the spiritual world than we do today in our modern, materialistic way of life.

So, when we become Christians, we should not be surprised to find that God breaks through the natural laws of this world, and gives us 'supernatural' experiences which are in fact the normal and natural way of life for the Christian living in the spiritual realm. These can range from answers to prayer to speaking in a spiritual language, or experiencing visions, prophecies, words of knowledge,

110

healings, dreams and miracles. Many sincere Christians feel that such supernatural manifestations do not form part of their Christian experience. I can only speak out of my own personal knowledge.

A friend confided to me that she wanted to explore the spiritual realm, but admitted to being afraid of anything that smacked of the supernatural. But we are not dealing with ghosts, or evil spirits, or things that go bump in the night; but with the Almighty God who is Spirit, and who seeks for people who will worship him in spirit and in truth (John 4.24). My friend's fear will greatly hinder her from receiving the gift of tongues, or being given a prophecy, or a word of knowledge, if God wants to use her in these ways. If we constantly remind ourselves that the gifts of the Spirit are a natural part of the spiritual realm which we have entered, we should be able to conquer any misgivings we may have, for 'to set the mind on the Spirit is life and peace' (Romans 8.6).

VISIONS

Vision, noun. Thing seen in dream; supernatural or prophetic apparition, phantom; thing seen in the imagination.

Acts 9.10: The Lord said to him in a vision . . .

Visions and dreams were frequently used by God in Old Testament times to speak to his people. They did not dismiss them, as we might, but believed that they were a direct message from God. Sometimes God spoke through angels, or later through the prophetic words of men who were in a position to listen to him. We can read how God used visions to speak to Abraham (Genesis 15.1), Isaiah (Isaiah 1.1; 6.1), Daniel (Daniel 10.1) and Nahum (Nahum 1.1).

Such dramatic forms of communication were not confined to Old Testament times. The prophecy in Joel chapter 2, that when the Spirit comes in the last days, so too will dreams, prophecies and visions, was fulfilled after the

111

ascension of Christ into heaven (Acts chapter 2). The Spirit was indeed poured out on to men and women, and the book of Acts has many accounts of visions which transformed the lives of individuals, and nations, as the recipients acted on them. What if Peter had not responded to his dream on the roof-top (chapter 10), or if Paul had disregarded the call from the man from Macedonia to 'Come over and help us' (16.9)?

Peter's experience is an interesting example of God speaking to two separate people in visions concerning the same matter. An 'angel of God' appeared to Cornelius, a centurion, telling him to send to Joppa to find Peter. The very next day, Peter was praying on the housetop while waiting for his lunch, when 'he fell into a trance'. God gave him a vision of a great sheet let down from heaven containing all kinds of animals and reptiles and birds, which he was commanded to kill and eat. Peter, as a good Jew, refused at first, for it was against the law for him to eat some of the animals he saw. But the voice continued: 'What God has cleansed, you must not call common.' To impress the message upon Peter, God gave him the vision three times.

The Bible says that 'Peter was inwardly perplexed'. What an understatement! But all was made clear, for almost immediately the envoys from Cornelius arrived at his gate. The Spirit told Peter to go down and without hesitation accompany these Gentiles back to the centurion, to whom he preached the gospel of Jesus.

So, because one man recognised God's voice through a rather strange vision, the message of Jesus as Saviour became available to all nations – to the Gentiles – and not just the Jews. In confirmation of this the Holy Spirit was poured out on the Gentile believers, signifying that God accepted them just as he did the Jewish people who believed in Jesus.

There may well be a few people in your fellowship who have the gift or ability to receive visions from the Lord (though I am sure he wants us all to be available to hear

112

from him in this way). Some people, too, have the gift of seeing 'pictures', often when they are praying, which when properly interpreted can convey a message from God. More and more, we are coming to respect such visions and pictures; but our problem seems to be in knowing what to do with them, and how to translate them. We know from Scripture that when someone speaks in tongues in a public meeting there should be an interpretation. In the same way, with a vision or picture, time should be spent in waiting on the Lord to ask him for the meaning. This needs careful and sensitive handling by the leader of a meeting or service, but such pictures or visions should certainly not be dismissed or left undealt with. Much of the Bible comes to us in picture language or symbols (for instance the parables of Jesus), and a close study of these subjects will help us as we seek to translate modern-day pictures and visions.

DREAMS

Dream, noun. Vision, series of pictures or events, presented to sleeping person; act, time, or seeing such vision.

Job 33. 14–16 (AV): For God speaketh once, yea twice, yet man perceiveth it not. In a dream, in a vision of the night . . . he openeth the ears of men.

Job 33.14–16 (RSV): For God speaks . . . in a dream, in a vision of the night . . . he opens the ears of men.

If our spiritual ears are a bit deaf, or we are not properly tuned in to the Lord, he can use our dreams to speak to us. We do not usually think about dreams as a way of listening to God, and it is only recently that western Christians have begun to realise that God still uses this method of speaking to us today. In some parts of the world it is taken for granted.

The Bible is full of stories of people who had dreams, and acted on them. As a supreme example, if Joseph had not obeyed his dream to take Mary and the infant Jesus down to Egypt, Jesus would have been killed by Herod. Other famous dreamers, from the Old and New Testaments, are Joseph the son of Jacob, Nebuchadnezzar, the Wise Men, Saul, Peter, and Pilate's wife. God spoke to Aaron and Miriam using dreams (Numbers 12.6–8); and he blessed Daniel by not only interpreting Nebuchadnezzar's dream, but also revealing it through the supernatural gift of knowledge (Daniel 4).

So God frequently used dreams as a medium of revelation, and he still does (Acts 2.17, quoting Joel 2). We may not necessarily have prophetic-type dreams that reveal something of the future; mostly our dreams will tell us something we need to know about ourselves. Very often (as in Job 33.12–18), they are to give us warnings of a wrong action or deed so that we may turn aside and change our ways. In fact, ninety-nine per cent of all dream material is about the dreamers themselves! Even when we dream about someone else, the dream is telling us about something in that person's character which is like our own.

The word for dream, *chalom* or *chalam*, is closely related to the Aramaic and Hebrew verb 'to be made healthy or strong'. Dreams thus provide a helpful picture of what is going on inside us. They can reveal what we are worrying about, what we should focus our attention on, and what needs sorting out in our lives. We live one tenth in the conscious world, but nine-tenths of our lives are deeply buried in the subconscious, along with all our fears, repressed hopes, psychological traumas etc. Dreams help to keep our inner selves clean and in order. They bring hidden things to the surface so that we can deal with them. Dreams are necessary to our health, for it has been shown that when people are deprived of them they become tired, distraught, inactive and irritable. So everyone dreams – whether they can remember them or not.

As Christians, by remembering our dreams and examining them in God's presence, we can have a whole new area of our personality – our subconscious – revealed to us. By bringing our dreams to the Lord in our quiet time, deep and hidden layers of hurt and other problems can be dealt with, confessed and healed. If we meditate on our dreams before the Lord, he can give us the interpretation and show us what they mean. When young Joseph was in prison in Egypt, the king's butler and baker came to him for an explanation of their dreams: 'We have had dreams and there is no one to interpret them.' Joseph's answer was immediate: 'Do not interpretations belong to God?' (Genesis 40.5–8).

It can be very rewarding to remember our dreams and consider whether the Lord is using them to say something to us; but we must take care not to get too carried away and spend more time analysing them than we do on our devotions! The way to remember dreams is to write them down immediately upon waking, or the majority of the dream will be lost after five or ten minutes. Writing them down helps to imprint them on our memory, and we can then use our notes for study and meditation before the Lord. We should include in our notes major events that are happening in our lives at the time (our current state of health, marriage, job situation etc.) so that we have a framework for our dreams. It is also helpful to share your dreams with your husband or a close friend. In Daniel 7.1 we read that Daniel 'wrote and told' – two helpful ways of remembering our dream material.

I mentioned earlier my experience of healing of the memories in relation to my father. On the following three consecutive nights, I had specific dreams about my father. On the first night I dreamed I was washing the floor of his bungalow; the second night I dreamed I was polishing the floor, and in the third and final dream I was polishing the doors and handles of an old village church, then opening the doors and seeing everything bright and shining inside. This was a clear indication to me from the Lord that a deep work of healing had indeed occurred after the prayer for healing of the memories.

If we allow him to, God will use our dreams to speak to

us, and as he interprets them we will be able to work out his salvation through areas of our lives that have hitherto remained deep and hidden.

WORDS OF WISDOM AND KNOWLEDGE

Wisdom, noun. Being wise, (possession of) experience and knowledge together with the power of applying them critically or practically, sagacity, prudence, common sense; wise sayings.

Knowledge, noun. Knowing, familiarity gained by experience (*of* person, thing, fact); person's range of information; theoretical or practical understanding (*of* subject, language, etc.); the sum of what is known.

1 Corinthians 12.8: To one is given through the Spirit the utterance of wisdom, and to another the utterance of knowledge according to the same Spirit.

It may seem strange to talk about wisdom and words of knowledge and a counselling ministry in the context of our quiet times. But God does not necessarily wait till we are in a counselling situation to reveal something to us. We may well be praying for someone in our quiet time and find that the Lord gives us a word of knowledge for that person which we can then pass on later.

Wisdom and knowledge are very important gifts and are part of the two-way flow between the Lord and ourselves. We need to be wise in dealing with people and helping them in the many problems that face us today, and many doctors and social workers probably have this gift in a worldly sense. Yet we need supernatural wisdom and the supernatural words of knowledge really to get to grips with many of the problems people have. Sometimes a counsellor who cannot make progress with an individual, receives a word of knowledge from the Lord which gives an important clue to what is blocking or hindering that person's recovery or healing.

Once my vicar let me sit in with him as he counselled a friend of mine. I sat back quietly most of the time, but when we were delving into this woman's past we hit a blockage, and the Lord gave the solution to me via a word of knowledge. This was simply 'white socks'. When I looked down at her feet, I realised that this woman, married with two children, was wearing white ankle socks. When I tentatively shared this, my vicar realised immediately that this was the key to unlock her past, for she still wanted to be a little girl and not grow up. When this was explained to her, she herself saw the socks as a clue to her behaviour and attitudes, and after confession and prayer during the following weeks I saw a great change in her, and a new and deeper relationship forming with her husband.

We read in Genesis 2.9 how Adam and Eve were tempted to take and eat of the fruit from the tree of knowledge. They were tempted to desire to be wise like God; but they tried to take such knowledge and wisdom by force. Now we have the tremendous promise from God that he will freely give this gift to those who ask: 'If any of you lacks wisdom, let him ask God, who gives to all men generously and without reproaching' (James 1.5).

PROPHECY

Prophecy, noun. Faculty of a prophet; prophetic utterance; fore-telling of future events.

Prophesy, verb. Speak as a prophet, foretell future event; expound the Scriptures.

Prophet, noun. Inspired teacher, revealer or interpreter of God's will.

1 Corinthians 14.4: He who prophesies edifies the church.

Prophecy is still a mystery to many Christians, and we look with awe on any in our fellowships who seem to have this supernatural gift. But again, though we are told that prophecy is for the edification and building up of the Church, the preparation for receiving and using such a gift will of necessity begin in our quiet times. We cannot expect

117

to see and hear and speak the mind of God in a prophetic way if we have not first spent time with him, especially in allowing him to speak to us first. He can give a word of prophecy through anyone who is willing to be used in this way, and who has tuned his ear to hear what the Lord is saying. As the definitions make clear, prophecy is not just telling forth a future event, such as we often see in the Old Testament and in the Book of Revelation; it is also expounding the Scriptures, and bringing to the Church the thoughts and words of God for present-day situations.

In Old Testament times, God needed prophets to speak to his people and he restricted himself to using those upon whom his Spirit especially rested – prophets, priests and kings. But now the Spirit has been poured out on all believers, and 'your sons and daughters *shall* prophecy'. The importance of prophecy is stressed in the Book of Proverbs: 'Where there is no prophecy the people cast off restraint' (Proverbs 29.18).

As our situations and circumstances change, we need to keep hearing the word of God for the here and now; last year's prophecy may not be applicable to today's situation. God is continually revealing himself, so he still needs prophets today. Those who feel called to this ministry may well feel alone, and therefore need the special love and support of their fellowship if they are to continue hearing and speaking out God's word. For this reason it is important for a person who exercises the prophetic gift to be related to a body of believers, and to be accountable to the local leaders. Some wise counsel that has been given to those who use this gift includes:

(a) Speak in tongues as much as possible and meditate on God's Word; this will 'tune you in' to hear from God.

(b) Start where you are. We are all priests to minister to each other, so we can all pass on to each other what we feel the Lord is saying.

(c) Start practising; pluck up courage and speak out, and allow the Lord to give you his word.

(d) Prophesy according to your faith.

(e) Make yourself available by spending plenty of time with the Lord.

(f) Study the prophetic Scriptures.

(g) Actually dare to ask the Lord, 'What is on your heart today? Do you have a word for me, or for my church?'

I learnt much of this when I went on a prophetic course a few years ago with a group of young people. I was by far the oldest one there, and felt rather conspicuous in my skirt and jumper amongst their jeans! Yet I was amazed to find it was not just in dress that I was the odd one out; for out of the twenty-five to thirty young people present, only I and one or two others had had no experience of prophesying. Since then I have begun to move forward tentatively in this area, and was very surprised (though I should not have been) when the Lord did give me prophecies when I waited on him. Of course, I passed them on to my church leaders, who in turn shared them with the fellowship.

Paul says (1 Corinthians 14) that we can all prophesy, one by one, so that all may learn and all be encouraged, and he even goes on to say (verse 39) that we should 'earnestly desire' to prophesy. A similar thought also comes from the Old Testament, where Moses says, 'I would that all the Lord's people were prophets, that the Lord would put his Spirit upon them' (Numbers 11.29).

Prophecy is a gift of the Holy Spirit, and an essential part of our full church life; but if we are to use this gift, we first need the preparation in our quiet times to enable us to speak out. Prophecy should be a normal and natural part of our life together, and as we grow closer to the Lord and more mature, then we should expect to see the Lord using more people in this way. Not only that – we should also be expecting the Lord to use us!

119

PRACTICAL

1 Using your concordance and cross-references, make a study of dreams, visions and prophecy in Scripture.
2 Buy a notebook and start to keep a record of your dreams, and use them as additional material for meditation in your quiet time.
3 Wisdom is personified in Scripture. Study the following passages for more information: 1 Corinthians 1.24 and 30, also the whole of the book of Proverbs.

PRAYER

Father, I pray that you will help me to be open to receiving through supernatural means your words, thoughts and knowledge. Thank you that you are Spirit, and that you dwell within me through your Holy Spirit. Help me to make myself available so that you can use me to speak to my fellowship. Amen.

BOOKS FOR FURTHER READING

George Mallone, *Those Controversial Gifts* (Hodder and Stoughton).
Morton Kelsey, *Dreams, a Way to Listen to God* (Paulist Press).
Catherine Marshall, *Something More* (Hodder and Stoughton).
Herman Riffel, *Your Dreams, God's Neglected Gift* (Kingsway).
John A. Sandford, *Dreams and Healing* (Paulist Press).

15

Dealing with Hindrances

Every Christian will face many temptations to stop spending time with God, and as the years pass it is all too easy for the world to 'squeeze us into its mould', as J. B. Phillips translates Romans 12.2. Some Christians do experience a time of 'backsliding', when they lose their first initial enthusiasm for the Lord, and, like the church in Laodicea, become neither hot or cold – only lukewarm (Revelation 3.14–16).

For a new Christian is may seem strange to be suddenly plunged into a new lifestyle that centres round God instead of yourself. You may find it hard initially to begin to read your Bible and pray; that is why it is so helpful to understand the importance of having a regular quiet time. Even for an older Christian who has missed out on quiet times for several weeks or even months, there will be a certain amount of lethargy to overcome in order to begin again. This is because the flesh is always warring against the Spirit (Galatians 5.17). If we are in this position, we will probably find that various things will stop us from actually getting down to our desired objective. It will therefore be helpful to look specifically at some of these hindrances, for forewarned is forearmed.

Such problems emanate from three main areas – described as the flesh, the world and the devil.

By 'the flesh' we mean our old human nature. First, we must straight away take stock of ourselves and recognise that a lack of enthusiasm or desire is one of the root causes of inadequate and ineffective quite times. Very often we don't have a quiet time simply because we don't want to, or we just can't be bothered. This sort of attitude has to be identified and changed. Once we are aware of it we can do something about it. And the first thing is to confess our lukewarmness to the Lord, and ask him to re-create in us a desire for his company, believing that he will certainly do so, as it is his will for us already.

An event which re-created my own enthusiasm for spending time with the Lord was a visit to our church by Dr John Coleman, one of the missionaries who had been imprisoned in Iran in the early 1980s. He told us that while in prison they had studied 2 Corinthians, which they found particularly suitable to their situation and needs. His testimony was such a stir to my faith that I decided that I also would study Paul's second letter to the Corinthians. I found that it brought me much blessing and practical help in my daily life, and whetted my appetite to go on to deeper study of other Scriptures.

So, one way of re-creating desire is by being with other Christians, and catching some of their enthusiasm. We can also look for the opportunity to ask our fellow Christians to pray with us and encourage us to cultivate a greater desire to spend time with the Lord. The writer to the Hebrews says that believers should 'Stir up one another' (Hebrews 10.24). Even airing the subject openly with others helps. I discovered as I initially talked to people that it was almost a taboo subject with a lot of Christians, mostly due to shame at not having a devotional time.

While at this moment we may be at the stage of needing to be stirred up ourselves, the time will undoubtedly come when we will be in a position to stir up others. This will be especially relevant if we are parents, for we will be doing our children a great service if they see us being enthusiastic and self-disciplined about spending time alone with God. The best way of doing this is for them to see our example, and for it to be a matter of family knowledge when parents are having a quiet time. Better still is for us to show a child how to have his own time with God, and go through some of the elements with him. When my eldest daughter was about twelve, she and I used to spend Monday evenings alone together, reading, praying and singing. She then felt able to share her innermost fears and worries with me, and they proved to be very precious hours. Such sharing on our part sets a good pattern for later life. Bible reading notes can be bought to suit children of all ages, and are often invaluable in developing the young mind towards an awareness of God. I can remember that I used to spend a few minutes in set Bible reading and prayer each night for at least a year before I actually became a Christian.

As I mentioned earlier, it is so often our own laziness, lack of desire, apathy and lack of self discipline that stops us from making the effort and finding time for God. These feelings need to be recognised, acknowledged, then confessed. Then we need to ask for renewal in this area of our thinking. 'Be renewed in the spirit of your minds' (Ephesians 4.23). This verse led me to think of my brain as filled with different memory tapes. I pictured myself taking out the tape that had imprinted on it 'Lack of enthusiasm' and 'Lack of desire and self-discipline', and replacing it with a tape which had imprinted on its circuits a new love and zeal for the things of God, and a new self-discipline in the matter of quiet times. I found that visualising the verse in this way greatly enhanced my understanding, so that it became true in fact, and not just wishful thinking on my part.

I have also found that reading about the lives and experiences of other Christians creates a thirst in me to seek the Lord more. At first I found many of these Christians' lives almost 'super-spiritual' and beyond my reach, but I realised that I ought not to be put off by thinking in this way, for we all have the capacity to live fully in the Spirit. We do, however, have to work actively at creating the initial desire to have a quiet time, or re-creating it after a period of absence.

It is also easy to feel guilty about missing out for so long, and to make that an excuse not to start; but again, it is important and beneficial to confess the situation to the Lord and to be honest with him about our feelings. Then it may be a question of gritting our teeth and beginning, no matter how hard we may find it, or how little we feel like it. No one is actually going to say to us, 'You must have a quiet time,' but we've already seen the blessings that follow, and that alone should be sufficient stimulus to make us take action.

The 'world' will also impinge on the time we could and should spend with God. The little book of Jude has some thing to say about this: 'In the last time there will be scoffers, following their own ungodly passions. It is these who set up divisions, worldly people, devoid of the Spirit. But you, beloved, build yourself up on your most holy faith . . . pray in the Holy Spirit' (Jude 18).

Scoffers may tempt us not to bother with a quiet time, and so prevent us from growing in the Lord and from prayer. This may well be the sort of situation that young Christians in college or university have to face, especially when there is such a lot happening around them that can easily squeeze out all thoughts and time for God. I have even heard it said by some Christian students that to have a quiet time regularly is to be bound by 'law', so they don't bother to have a daily time with the Lord, not wishing to be held under such bondage!

Of course, slavishly following a set pattern of quiet times year in and year out would be very boring and uninspiring; but quiet times need not be repetitious. By adding variety we do indeed add that necessary 'spice' to our encounter with the Lord that makes us thirst for more. If we just have toast or cereals for breakfast every day we will soon be-come bored – even though the food may be doing us good. It's a simple matter to add variety to spiritual 'breakfasts' too, so that not only do we know they are benefiting our health and giving us strength and energy, we can also enjoy the process at the same time. God wants us to enjoy our quiet times, not to see them as something that must be endured.

It only takes a few minutes thinking through an average day to discover other pressures that will try and stop us finding time for God. Work may take up a large part of the day; and of course we must do our jobs well and faithfully serve our employers. For some, however, their job takes a far too important position in their lives, and they either spend long hours in overtime, or else bring work home, to the detriment of their relationship with the Lord – and their families.

Another area to look at is our leisure time. Just how much television do we watch? How long do we spend reading library books, magazines, the newspaper? And what about our hobbies? I have always loved to sew, and being rather small, it has often been necessary to make my own clothes. About four years ago, the Lord showed me that my sewing was becoming too important in my life and taking up too much of my time. I had allowed something in my life to get completely out of proportion, and so the Lord said 'no more', till I had learned to view it in a right perspective. When it was no longer so important in my life the Lord allowed me to take it up again.

It is all a question of priorities, and what we feel is important in our lives. Very few of the pressures of the world are wrong in themselves – it is how we view them and what we do with them that shows God where our first love is – for him, or them?

Our biggest hindrances are caused by the devil, for he will do his utmost to stop us growing in the faith. He is delighted when we cease to grow as Christians due to hindrances from ourselves, or from our busy lives. But if we stand up to these influences and overcome them, he may well try other tactics, sometimes openly, sometimes more subtly, and we need to be on the lookout for such attacks. 'Be watchful', warns Peter. 'Your adversary the devil prowls around like a roaring lion seeking someone to devour. Resist him' (1 Peter 5.8).

Paul experienced this, as he relates in his letter to the Thessalonians. He tried again and again to visit them, 'but Satan hindered us (1 Thessalonians 2.18). But against this, we have the lovely promise in James 4.7: 'Submit yourselves to God. Resist the devil and he will flee from you.'

God has also provided other means for our protection from Satan – by giving us his armour. A description of this is in Ephesians chapter 6. It was a great revelation to me when I found out how to appropriate to myself these extremely important verses. Again I use my imagination, to picture myself putting on each piece of armour, and prayerfully going through each item and its meaning.

I place the helmet of salvation on my head, praying that the Lord will keep me safe, especially in the area of my mind and my thoughts – the places Satan loves to attack! Then I put the breastplate of righteousness on my chest, thanking God that his righteousness protects me. This piece of armour is especially important as it protects our emotions and stops them going astray. I then place the belt of truth around my waist, so that not only will I speak and act the truth, but also walk in it.

I then put my feet into the shoes of the gospel of peace. I find this especially helpful when I am going into new situations, for I picture my footsteps as being new territory gained for the Lord, and with each footstep I can proclaim 'peace, peace.'

When our son began a new school, a teacher who was a Christian took us round, showing us the classrooms, the assembly hall and so on. As we walked round, we consciously brought the Lord's peace with each footstep we took, taking him into every room and area. In this way we claimed new territory for God, just as the priests did as the Israelites crossed the river Jordan into the land of promise (Joshua 3.13).

126

The next item of the armour is a shield. The Roman soldier carried a large, long shield, which when held up in front of him completely covered and protected his body. Bible verses such as 'The Lord is my strength and shield' (Psalm 28.7) come alive for us when we picture this and see it as God's provision for our protection from all the flaming darts of the enemy. The Roman shields were made of such hard wood that they actually did stop the burning arrows of the enemy from taking hold. An added advantage of the Roman shield was that a group or company of soldiers attacking an enemy fort could raise their shields together over their heads and so provide a 'roof' for protection and covering for themselves and each other.

Lastly, I picture myself handling the sword, which is the word of God. This, of course, is another reason why we need to be thoroughly acquainted with the Bible, so that we can use it to defend ourselves, as well as to attack. After his forty day fast in the wilderness, Jesus was tempted by the devil in three different areas of his life, and each time he used Scripture to confound and rebuke him. At the same time he showed us by example how to use it effectively, for it did indeed become active and living, just like the two-edged sword described in Hebrews 4.12.

Sometimes the devil attacks the Christian openly. I can remember, when I was in my first job as a young Christian, that I was delighted to be working with an older girl who was really mature in the Lord and well grounded in Scripture. It amazed me when one day she explained that for two or three days she had been physically unable to open her mouth and pray. That was over twenty years ago, and neither of us knew then about resisting the devil and binding him (Mark 3.27) She knew enough, however, to recognise it as a Satanic attack, and presumably someone prayed with her, for she was soon able to pray for herself again.

Satan does not usually attack so directly though, but often tries more subtle means of deflecting us from the faith. After I first received the fullness of the Spirit, I had two or three really frightening dreams about snakes chasing me up and down a tall building. When I shared this with my vicar he explained that the devil was trying to make me believe that nothing had happened, especially as I didn't have any outward confirmation to begin with. But he also counselled me that the devil would not have tried to frighten me subtly if there had been no cause; so in fact this experience only confirmed my new awareness of the Holy Spirit.

One of the keys to resisting Satanic attacks is to recognise them in the first place. The ability to recognise when Satan is 'seeking to devour us' will come as we grow and mature in the Lord.

When he was here on earth, Jesus had full authority to cast out the devil and demons that possessed people. But he also passed that authority and power on to his disciples when he sent them out (Matthew 10.1). More wonderfully still, the Bible teaches that we have full authority here on earth to do the same works as Jesus – in fact even greater (John 14.12). So we can take the name of Jesus, the name at which every knee must bow, and bind Satan from hindering us in any way. Once we are clothed with God's armour, we are then adequately protected and enabled to bind the strong man and resist him.

PRACTICAL

Draw a small picture of a Roman soldier wearing all the parts of the armour of God, and keep it in a prominent place to remind you to put it on. You may find a picture to copy from an encyclopaedia – or you could get a friend to draw it if you're not artistic! If that too is difficult, then write each piece of the armour down on card or paper and keep it near you, so that you can at least read it and appropriate each piece, to yourself.

PRAYER

Father, I thank you that though temptations to stay away from your presence will come, through the flesh, the world and the devil, you have given me ample protection and covering to cope with them. Help me to so appropriate your Word that it becomes really meaningful in my life, and enables me to gain the victory in your name.   Amen.

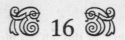

16

Going on Retreat

The dictionary definition of a retreat implies a removal or moving away, but for the Christian the word can have a totally new meaning – that of moving forward.

But there is no point in moving forward if there are things left behind us undone, or not done correctly, or not even learned in the first place. Most Christians find it essential to go back to the Cross at various times in their lives, to reaffirm their first love and commitment, to experience again the wonder of Jesus's death and resurrection, and to make sure that all their burdens and sins have been left at the Cross and not picked up again.

So we may initially take a step back, but it is only in order to move forward positively, with new aims and desires within us, and a greater awareness of the Lord in our lives.

Going on a retreat is one way of showing the Lord our willingness to retire from the world for a while, from all the distractions that would hinder our walk with him. Making the effort to go away gives us a chance to look at ourselves without the hustle and business of the everyday routine, so that we can reappraise our life, direction and hopes, and set new patterns and goals for the future. A retreat is not a negative drawing back from problems or difficulties, but a chance to face them realistically and do something about sorting them out.

Retreats can have a similar effect to fasting. We go without a meal so that we can spend more time with God and show him our heart's intentions. In the same way, setting aside a day, or several days, to wait exclusively upon

God, means that we are giving up something else – namely our time.

There are various ways of going on retreat. The ideal is to be on our own, for then the Lord has more opportunity to speak to us and we are not distracted by having other people around. Another form of retreat is to go away with one other person, perhaps spending some part of the day alone and then coming together to compare notes, to pray and to minister to each other. It can also be helpful to go away with a group of Christians, on a church weekend house-party for instance. Retreats taken with other people will have different benefits from going away on one's own, but are still of great value. There is much to learn through the joy and companionship of being with each other, through times of worship and praise, and the opportunity to hear new things – perhaps from a guest speaker. It is also possible for an individual to join closed or open retreats, where there is a conducted programme structured round talks and worship. Other retreats may deal with specific areas such as healing, prayer, commitment, the family, silence, or marriage encounter.

The effects of a retreat will be long-term, probably extending into years. Jesus experienced this, for he in particular knew the value of being alone with his Father. Immediately after he received the baptism in the Holy Spirit he was driven by that same Spirit out into the wilderness – a form of retreat. For our Lord this was a time of testing and proving and temptation. But he returned from his wilderness experience strengthened with the knowledge that he was able to resist the tempter, and was filled with power for his subsequent ministry (Luke 4.1–15).

Another after-effect of a retreat can be a new desire to work for God, as well as the ability to complete that work. We see from the story of Jesus and the disciples on the Mount of Transfiguration (again another kind of retreat), that when he came down he was immediately faced with the demands of a father for his epileptic child, and was able to perform a work of healing.

Moses, too, had what we would call mountain-top experiences, and was immediately involved in action on his return from them (Exodus 24.15–18). On one occasion when he came down from the mountain he was faced with a situation of grave sin on the part of the people, and he had to stand firm and show the people there and then the importance of the two tablets of stone he held in his hands – the Commandments (Exodus 32).

After a prolonged time spent with God, other people may be aware that something about us is different. We saw earlier that the second time Moses came down from the mountain, after receiving the new tablets of stone, he 'did not know that the skin of his face shone because he had been talking with God' (Exodus 34.29).

What are the circumstances which may lead us to want to go on retreat?

1 When we first come to the Lord. This seems to have been Paul's experience. He hints in Galatians 1.17–18 that after spending a few days with the disciples after his conversion (Acts 9) he then went into Arabia, which is a desert, and did not join the other disciples in Jerusalem for three years. It seems that he spent this considerable time alone, consolidating his new-found faith, sorting out his ideas and realigning them in the light of his experience of Jesus, and generally waiting upon God.

2 When we are seeking God's will for something specific. Esther is a good example of this, for though she did not actually go on a retreat, she saw the necessity of fasting and praying for three days to prepare herself to go into the king and plead for her people – the Jews (Esther 4.15–17).

3 When we are seeking for a new awareness of the Lord, or for his gifts. Ten years ago Peter went away on a retreat to a monastery for a whole weekend. He went with the

specific aim of reaffirming his love for the Lord, and recommitting his life, as well as to seek for the fullness of the Spirit. He received the latter experience towards the end of his time away, while on his own in one of the monks' cells.

4   To gain strength for a difficult task ahead. This is highlighted by the experience of Jesus when he spent time in the Garden of Gethsemane prior to the Cross.

5   When we are afraid, for ourselves, about the future, about ill health, and so on. Elijah the prophet also knew fear, and was so afraid of being killed by Jezebel that he ran away (1 Kings 19.1–18). He 'went a day's journey into the wilderness', and was in such dire straits that he was suicidal. But the Lord met him there, and he was fed and given strength to return to face his prophetic duties.

6.   At the beginning of a new job or ministry. Our curate and his wife, a deaconess, were ordained at the same time and were together on the two-day pre-ordination retreat. She shared with us how she found the silence an especially welcome occasion to reflect over the training of the previous seven years after her call to the ministry. It was also a time to assess her feelings and to anticipate what the future might hold, and to examine her life and where she might have to be flexible and ready to change her ideas.

7   When we need to make a decision. We read in Luke 6.12 that Jesus went out to a mountain to pray, and continued in prayer to God all night. The following morning he came down from the mountain and immediately chose his twelve disciples. So he was obviously seeking his Father's guidance during those night hours alone.

We may have no particular reason for going on a retreat, except perhaps that we feel that the Lord is calling us aside. Moses, before God called him to lead Israel, spent forty years in the wilderness, mostly on his own, looking after the sheep. Yet even from this job he 'turned aside' because something attracted his attention (Exodus 3). We are usually so busy and so caught up with outside pressures that we may have little time for God. A retreat is an ideal opportunity for us just to be with the Lord, being still and waiting upon him.

So, what can we do on a retreat to make the best use of the time available? If we look on it as an extended and enlarged version of our quiet times, we can see that all the elements we use in our devotions can also be used on a retreat. The joy of being away, though, is that we can spend far longer on each aspect.

Whatever form of retreat we choose, it will be more rewarding if we prepare well in advance, and plan a time-table. If we go with a group, there will probably be scheduled times for talks, periods on our own, meals and light recreation. If we go on our own, we need to include meals (unless we are fasting), drinks and relaxation as part of the structure, but concentrate the majority of our time on being with the Lord.

For example, we could spend the first half-hour in praise and worship, followed by half an hour's Bible study. The next period could be spent in silence, quietly waiting on God. Then we could break for a drink, and come back to prayer and intercession, followed maybe by a time of thinking through a particular issue that we need to sort out. It is helpful, too, to take some literature, perhaps on the same issue for which we are seeking guidance. Finally, we must not forget to take the other tools such as notebook, pen, hymn book, concordance, etc. Preparing a plan before hand concentrates our minds before we go away, and is one way of ensuring that we gain the maximum benefit.

If we go away with one other person it is still a good idea to have a structure planned (and to make sure that any such plan is agreed by both parties!) in advance, especially as it is easy to get distracted from our main purpose by idle chatter and conversation.

If we are with lots of other people we need to be aware of their needs as well as our own. Going away with a group usually means that there is little time for an extensive period of silent meditation or study, yet most Christian hotels or house-party venues have a quiet room or chapel available, and if we discipline ourselves it is possible to make sure we spend some time alone with the Lord.

One of the problems, after deciding to have a retreat, is finding a place to go. Our church elders spend a day away with each other once or twice a year, and they use another local church as their venue. A friend and I once borrowed someone's house in the country for a day of prayer and waiting on God. There are also many Christian hotels and guest houses all round the country which have suitable facilities. Probably the best places to provide the ideal surroundings of peace and quietness are convents or monasteries; many of them have opportunities for people to stay on a retreat basis. We can watch the advertisements in the Christian press for details of such venues, or maybe our church leaders will have addresses we can write to.[1]

Another thing to bear in mind about retreats is that not only are they good for us as individuals, but we ought also to be on the lookout for others who may be in desperate need of such a time, and to whom we can offer help and advice. The story of the woman in 2 Kings chapter 4 comes to mind. She specially prepared a room for Elisha on the roof of her house, so that he had somewhere to stay when he was in her area. An army couple in our church have often made their home available during the week to people in need while they were staying in army quarters on the base. If we find ourselves in a position to encourage someone to go away on retreat, we should also think about showing them how to get the most value out of it. In some situations it may even be right to suggest that we go with them. Not only will the other person be helped, but we, too, will be blessed as we share ourselves in this way.

But however much we may desire to go on a retreat, for

some of us it may just not be possible. As an alternative, we can try to arrange a mini-retreat in our own homes. If you are at work during the day, then perhaps you could set aside one whole evening to spend with the Lord, following some of the suggestions already made. If you are at home, perhaps you could arrange with your partner, or a friend, to have the children on a Saturday morning or afternoon for an extended time of getting away from it all. Once the Lord puts the desire within us, there will always be a way to solve the problem of when and where, especially if we are willing to seek advice and help from others.

PRACTICAL

Ask yourself if you need to go away for an extended time with the Lord. If the answer is yes, then start making enquiries and practical decisions as to when and where.

PRAYER

Father, I pray that you will show me when the time is right for me to spend an extended time with you. Please help me with the practical details, and prepare my heart to receive you in a deeper way.   Amen.

NOTE

1   Further information can be obtained from the Association for Promoting Retreats, Church House, Newtown Road, London W2 5LS. See also the following publications:

Geoffrey Gerard, *Away from it all*: A guide to retreat houses and monastic hospitality (Lutterworth Press).

George Target, *Out of This World*: A guide to religious retreats (Bishopsgate Press).

🎴 17 🎴

Action and Obedience

> Be doers of the word, and not hearers only, deceiving
> yourselves. For if any one is a hearer of the word and not a
> doer, he is like a man who observers his natural face in a
> mirror; for he observes himself and goes away and at once
> forgets what he was like. But he who looks into the perfect law,
> the law of liberty, and perseveres, being no hearer that forgets
> but a doer that acts, he shall be blessed in his doing.   (James
> 1.22–5)

If we want our quiet times really to affect and change our
relationship with God, then we need to think carefully
about obeying him and doing something positive about the
things we learn. In the passage quoted above, James is
speaking about a man who looked in the mirror, saw his
imperfections, his natural face, his natural nature, but then
went away and forgot what he was like and as a consequence did nothing about it. When we look in the heavenly,
two-way mirror, and see Jesus reflected there, we see the
son of God in his perfection; and such perfection as his
rapidly shows up our own sins, faults and failings. The man
referred to by James saw the things that were wrong in his
life, which the law of liberty revealed to him, but he forgot
to act on what he saw.

The Bible says that without the commandments, or the
law, the people did not know what it was to sin (Romans
7.7). But once they had a law that said: 'Do not steal,' they
then knew that stealing was wrong, and they either had to
stop stealing, or be guilty of breaking the law. In the same

way we can look in the mirror, into the same perfect law (God's word) and see the life of God lived perfectly in his son, the man Jesus Christ. We now have a heavenly standard by which to measure ourselves, and in so doing we realise that we fall short of his perfection. But it is no good looking in the mirror, seeing Jesus and wanting to be like him if we then walk away from our quiet times, forget all the things that Jesus has revealed to us, and do nothing about those areas of our lives that need changing.

An important criterion of our quiet times should be our willingness to obey God. If we ask him to speak to us (and there is no doubt that he will), we have to be prepared to do as he says. If we are disobedient, after a while we shall not even be able to hear his voice. This is because when we don't obey and act on what he says, then we become dull of hearing (Hebrews 5.11). God is still speaking to us, still trying to reach us; but we block our ears by active disobedience or passive inactivity. There is then the danger that God will cease speaking to us if he keeps getting no response, or if we take no action.

It is a spiritual law that the words of promise follow the actions of obedience. Time and time again in the Old Testament, obedience is linked with blessing. In fact the whole of Deuteronomy chapter 28 is based on his law: 'If you obey the voice of the Lord your God . . . , the Lord will set you on high above all the nations . . . and all these blessings shall come upon you' (verses 1–2). Every area of life was to receive God's blessing, from the children, to fields, herds, storehouses and Israel's relationship with other nations. Twelve verses of blessings! Sadly, there then follow over thirty verses of curses that would fall upon the Israelites if they disobeyed the Lord.

Obedience is far more important in God's eyes even than sacrifice (1 Samuel 15.22). It is no good, therefore, giving up every evening to go door-knocking or evangelising, leading a youth group or Sunday school class, fasting or tithing, if God has said to you, 'Forgive your neighbour

138

next door for not returning your mower', and in your heart of hearts you still bear resentment. Jesus said (Matthew 5.23): 'First put it right with your neighbour or brother – then bring your offering.' First obey and then act – then God accepts and he acts.

At the end of his life, Joshua called the people of Israel together and gave them a choice – either to serve the gods of the nations around them, or to serve and obey the Lord, who had brought them out of Egypt and had done marvellous things for them. Their reply was one which we should do well to echo: 'The Lord our God we will serve, and his voice we will obey' (Joshua 24.24).

The whole aim of this book has been to explore ideas on enlarging and enriching our quiet times, but it will not achieve its purpose if you just read it and forget it. You will only gain benefit and blessing if you start putting into practice as many as possible of the things you have learned.

An added bonus to be gained from using and practising many of the elements discussed, and other spiritual gifts, in our private devotions, is that we gain confidence in using them, and later we shall feel more able to use them in public. If we learn to raise our hands to the Lord in worship quietly at home, it will be much easier to do it in a service later on. If we get used to speaking in tongues, or pray for interpretation, in our quiet time, we shall feel more confident to do so in an open meeting. If we seek to study the Bible in greater depth, the Lord may well give us a teaching ministry.

A close friend and I wanted to move forward in the area of interpretation, so we got together on several occasions to pray in tongues. We were a bit shy about it at first, but grew more confident and at ease as we carried on speaking out our spiritual language – then waited to see if the Lord gave us an interpretation. We did this a few times, practising and experimenting. Several months later in a house group meeting someone else spoke in tongues, and my friend received and gave the interpretation. Practising and praying about it beforehand had enabled her to be open to the Lord and to speak out in public.

But it is not just the seemingly important or outwardly showy gifts that need experimenting with. A very shy woman in our house group began to read her Bible out loud at home in her quiet time. That year our group was asked to lead the service on Christmas morning. You can imagine the joy it was to the rest of us when she offered to stand up and read one of the lessons, which she subsequently did beautifully. After that she gained more confidence, and was able to pray at meetings and join more fully in the discussions.

It can be a great delight to watch others move forward into new spiritual experiences. I was blessed when a young girl in our church confided to me that she wanted to feel free about raising her hands in public; and that after practising in her quiet times, she specifically went to a local praise meeting with other churches so that she could join in the praise and raise her hands. Another of my friends, who has to wear a leg caliper, was sitting next to me during a praise meeting. At one point in the worship she and I stood up simultaneously, and she then leaned forward and picked up a tambourine from the chair in front and began to tap it. It was such a thrill to me to see her struggle to get up, having to clip her caliper into place, and then to stand and play an instrument to worship the Lord. I felt our hearts joined together at that moment, and it was a very special and precious time. Because she stood up, which took a real effort on her part, I in turn received a blessing.

We can see, then, that not only will we ourselves experience blessing as we obey the Lord and actively respond to him, but others in our fellowship and churches will also be blessed as we practise new ways of experiencing God in our quiet times, and begin to use them in the wider circle of our churches and fellowships.

PRACTICAL

Choose an element that you have recently added to your quiet time and begin to look for opportunities of using it within the context of a house group, prayer meeting or church.

PRAYER

I thank you, Father, that your Word is living and powerful, and that as I spend time with you my whole life will be changed. Help me to be both obedient and active in my Christian life, so that blessings may rebound on all around me. Amen.

18

The End Result

We saw at the beginning that God's aim for us is to make us like his son, Jesus Christ, and to unite his Holy Spirit with our spirits. We then become truly one with the living God – a 'mystery' as Paul says in Ephesians 1.9–10. The natural outcome is that as individual Christians we shall find we are growing up in the Lord and maturing. God desires to present the Church to his Son as a bride, ready for her bridegroom. But he does not want a weak, ineffective, powerless Church. He is seeking for a mature, grown-up, effective and powerful bride, who is fitted to rule alongside his Son in the heavenly realm.

We have already seen that our own desire plays an important part in the value we place on a devotional time with the Lord. We need to be infected with the same zeal as the apostle Paul, who wrote that he counted everything worldly as loss, 'because of the surpassing worth of knowing Christ Jesus my Lord'. He suffered the loss of all things that he 'might gain Christ and be found in him' and that he might 'know the power of his resurrection'. He saw life as a race, something he had to persevere in. All through his life he forgot what lay behind, and strained forward to what lay ahead, and so, at the end of his life, achieved his goal and received the prize of his upward call in Christ Jesus. (Philippians 3.7–16). Paul's encouragement to us would be the same as that of the prophet Hosea (in chapter 6.3): 'Let us know, let us press on to know the Lord.'

Christian growth and maturity come only from receiving spiritual food from the one who feeds us – God. Paul wanted to speak to the Corinthian church as to spiritual adults but unfortunately they were not ready for it. He still had to feed them the easy, elementary, first things, because they were still much 'of the flesh', giving way to jealousy and anger. They were behaving like 'ordinary men', not like redeemed sons of God (1 Corinthians 3.1–4). The writer to the Hebrew Christians says much the same thing. He wanted to go on to much deeper things with them. They ought to have reached the stage of teaching others, but he had still to continue feeding them with milk. Why? Because they were dull of hearing – they couldn't, or didn't, hear God's voice, and were unskilled in the word of righteousness, unable even to tell right from wrong – good from evil (Hebrews 5.11–14).

It takes both desire and effort to wean ourselves off milk and on to solid food. Picture yourself as a baby, lying in your mother's arms, taking milk from her breast or a bottle. How easy it is just lying there and sucking, or being spoon-fed with cereal or rusks! What a different picture emerges when we imagine ourselves grown-up, with a plate of meat, potatoes and vegetables placed before us. For a start we have to sit up, then use a knife and fork to cut the food, and carry it to our mouths. It takes effort – but the sight and smell of the food sets our mouths watering, and of course, the more we eat, the stronger we get. God has a wealth of solid spiritual food to give us, but we have to desire to grow up before we can start feeding ourselves with the deep things from his storehouse. God does not mean us to remain babies – he needs grown up sons and daughters who are mature enough to take on responsibility, and be given authority in their turn to feed others. He wants sons and daughters who are mature enough to take on the leadership and charge of his Church. So long as we stay immature, still needing to be fed the elementary basics of the Christian life, we are still accounted as children, having to be cared for, instead of caring for others.

As we as individuals grow and mature, we can see that the change in us has a snowball effect in our churches and fellowships. The more we strengthen and deepen our own spiritual lives, the stronger our brothers and sisters in Christ will become. As each Christian in a church or fellowship spends more time with the Lord, and uses his gifts, and naturally matures, so the life of the church is strengthened, and the whole body is built up. As we each learn from the Lord and become more like Jesus, we take our new growth and awareness into our fellowships, and they in turn are enriched. The church will only be as strong as the individual Christians that make up that body, as a chain is only as strong as its weakest link. If we are in a position of leadership or authority, it is even more important that we mature and press on to deeper things. A church as a whole can only move forward when its leaders press on to new heights.

It is helpful to see the Church pictured as a body, and to realise how each one of us is necessary to the functioning of that body. Some may have seen this visibly and powerfully portrayed as we did in our own church several years ago at a weekend house-party. Our curate had with him a large number of cards, and on each one was written the name of a different bone of the body. He then handed one card to each person present, and told us to move round the room till we found the next bone that joined with ours. We had to keep going until the whole body, or skeleton, was in position. It was great fun taking part in this, and as we were a large group of people, there were enough of us to take up the required number of bones. Later I took part in the same exercise with a much smaller house-party from another church, and it was amazing to stand by and watch the consternation on their faces as it dawned upon them that they could not complete the skeleton. Here and there vital parts of the bones, or body, were missing; and after the excitement and giggling and getting into position had subsided, it came as quite a shock to them to realise that there

144

were such large gaps. They then realised how necessary each person was in their church, no matter how small a part they played in the running or organisation.

For a church in its turn to grow and mature, it needs every part of the body to be together, for if one part is missing the whole suffers (1 Corinthians 12.14–26). If somebody has the gift of prophecy but stays away, then the whole church is denied the opportunity of hearing what the Lord has to say. The person who is especially good at welcoming visitors will be sorely missed if he does not turn up, as will those who sit quietly praying all through a service. If the people who do the flowers forget one Sunday, another facet of blessing is removed from the service; and if the members of the leadership do not attend the meetings, how will important decisions be made?

Here is where we see the ultimate importance of using and experimenting with the gifts and talents which God has given us, and putting into practice, in the wider framework of the church, the things he has taught us in our quiet time.

A couple of years ago our church house-groups studied the many gifts of the Lord. We discovered nearly thirty, including such varied things as celibacy, 'helps', mercy, pastoring, dance, and administration, as well as the more well-known and supernatural gifts. Looking through the list, it became obvious that most, if not all, of the gifts were for the blessing and benefit of the church, as well as for the individual recipient. The church in Ephesus had to learn that 'his gifts were . . . to equip the saints for the work of ministry, for the building up of the body of Christ, until we all attain to the unity of the faith and of the knowledge of the son of God, to mature manhood' (Ephesians 4.11–13). All our gifts and talents, and indeed many of the elements we can use in our quiet time, are for the blessing and benefit, the growth and maturity of the Church – the body of Christ. To each is given the manifestation of the Spirit

145

for the common good (1 Corinthians 12.7). The manifestations of the Spirit are the gifts which the Lord gives to you and me, but they are for the sake of the corporate body, for the common good of the fellowship of believers of which we are a part. Whether our gifts are natural, or supernatural, they are for the benefit of the person you and I sit next to in church, and for the whole body. In this way, the Church will benefit from the gifts that individuals bring, and in turn can move on to deeper things and mature.

'As each has received a gift, employ it for one another, as good stewards of God's varied grace' (1 Peter 4.10).

Many of the elements we have looked at come under the list of gifts, such as faith, intercession, tongues, prophecy, and so on. In addition many of the elements, which are not strictly gifts, can also be used to enhance our times of fellowship in our churches – praise and worship, singing, dancing, standing, praying. As we gain confidence and fluency in the use of these elements in our quiet time, so we can transfer their use to the wider context of the church; in this way everyone can have the opportunity to be uplifted, strengthened and encouraged. This is why it is so important to see our quiet times alone with God not just as an end in themselves, but as the springboard to a strong and mature church.

Paul's chief desire was to present 'every man mature in Christ' (Colossians 1.26–9), and he toiled with all his might and energy to achieve this end result. Let us aim to join him, through the means of our quiet times, in reaching mature manhood and womanhood for ourselves, and bodily growth and maturity for our churches and fellowships.

PRAYER

Father, I do desire to obey you, and to wean myself off the milk and on to the meat of your Word. Thank you that the Christian life is an ongoing experience and that I am daily growing and maturing as I spend time alone with you. Thank you for the church where I worship and serve; and I pray for its growth and maturity and for it to truly be the bride of Christ. Amen.

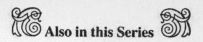

Creativity
Using your talents

EILEEN MITSON AND OTHERS

'In the beginning God created ...'
and we, his children, made in his image,
also have the desire to create.
Creativity is God's gift to us.

If therefore our lives are open to him,
he will show us areas in every aspect of life
in which we can create new growth –
our homes, families and environment,
in our relationships and in our own
personalities and talents.
He has already provided us with the raw materials –
we can use them to build or destroy –
we can choose to be on the side of life, or of death.

Nine women who have chosen life
have contributed to this thought provoking book,
which will inspire every Christian woman
to explore new ideas and to develop
her own unique creative potential.

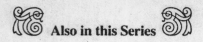

Also in this Series

A Woman's Privilege

JEAN BRAND

The modern Christian woman
is often confused about her place in the world.
Secular pressures have blurred the
divisions between male and female roles.
Is this in line with God's plan for women?
Or does he require a woman to submerge
her whole personality
in submission to her husband?
And what about single women?

Jean Brand affirms that the Bible
represents a far more glorious pattern
and shows in a practical way, how every woman
can use her individuality and experience
to become the person God intends her to be.

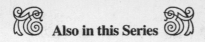

Also in this Series

Family Planning
The ethics and practicalities of birth control methods

GAIL LAWTHER

This Christian book on contraception
looks at the options available
and is intended for Christians
who are married or planning to marry
and who wish to regulate their fertility
in a way compatible with their faith.

Gail Lawther has researched the subject carefully
and discusses in a Christian light
the methods available, their practicalities, the risks
and the advantages and disadvantages of each.
Special attention is paid to the
ethical questions involved and to the
new problems raised for Christians
by some of the most recent research.
Couples who are concerned to make the right choices
with each other and before God will find her approach
particularly helpful and informative.

Also in this Series

Birthright?
A Christian woman looks at abortion
MAUREEN LONG

Like many Christian women,
Maureen Long is deeply concerned about
current permissive attitudes to abortion.
Her book reveals the enormous scale
of the problem, in terms of lives destroyed,
and also other less publicised aspects,
such as the long-term effects on the mother,
and potential family and social problems.
All these are discussed in the light
of the Bible's teaching about
the sacredness of life.

Birthright? calls on Christians
to fight for legal and social recognition
of every child's right to be born,
and gives practical suggestions about how
this can be done, including information
about pro-life societies and
organisations.

Other titles in preparation